FOR THOSE WHO ARE WILLING TO LISTEN READ ON

by
Sir Oliver Lodge and others

Spiritually Transcribed
by
Raymond Smith

Front cover by Richard E.Baddely

CON-PSY PUBLICATIONS MIDDLESEX

First Edition

© Raymond Smith
1998

ISBN 1 898680 11 6

Published by
CON-PSY PUBLICATIONS
P.O.BOX 14
GREENFORD
MIDDLESEX UB6 0UF

CONTENTS

FOREWORD

It is a well nigh impossible task perhaps to comment, never mind elaborate on the issues and details of this Ray's second book, the contents of which deal with many basic issues central to the understanding of our existence. In a sense those who inspire Ray (and are the true minds behind this thinking) I feel will forgive my inadequacies in these comments I have been kindly asked to write.

Readers who truly wish "to listen" will receive much inspiration from this further volume of writings from Oliver and his friends. There is much material to stimulate the mind, and indeed, as we are always learning; to question. You will find in this volume however the impact of Rays inspirers as they project their personalities, and express their thoughts through the pages. They elaborate upon much discussed and wondered material. Of particular interest to myself were the comments on the dream world, and the possible nature of our spiritual existence; but most of all it is the down to earth and solid nature of the material which can be most inspiring. Oliver Lodge and the other team members were influential people while on earth, and in a sense to many the wonderment that they exist after so called death still beggars the mind !

Such material calls for a quantum leap in our thinking, indeed Oliver and the other helpers would not wish us to accept everything said..we have our own views and free will. We need to make our own minds up, and this is the same with all survival evidence. One incident, one book, or experience may not constitute ultimate proof of survival to us; but just help us one step of the way to an understanding, and I know Oliver and the others would go along with this.

I have been fortunate indeed to question Oliver and his friends in some detail. I have both audio and video evidence of Oliver's return, but even then he was at pains to point out that even he; in all his talks and writings cannot provide many of us with personal proof. That is something he says we need to find for ourselves, and will remain very personal.

The return of Oliver, Charles, Franz, Phillipe and Harold; at least to the degree of sophistication needed to write this book has taken many years of dedicated development. It has been a privilege to be associated with Ray and June and all the other helpers myself and my wife have met. It is a rare event today to experience such trance development in mediums, and such consistency of thought from those in spirit. Anyone who has had the chance to question will probably soon realise that there are very sophisticated minds at work here, with gems of information which in my case both helped verify aspects of the communicators lives, and related to personal

4

details of which the medium had no knowledge.

For every question, I like you will probably have a hundred more! This volume goes in no short measure to try and penetrate into that understanding. As such it is a rare gem in the sea of so much mud that passes as survival literature today. I hope the reading of it will illuminate your understanding that little more. That is ultimately what the team would wish.

Malcolm Lewis
Fleetwood, England.
August 1997

Raymond Smith

PREFACE

Many years ago, a medium friend of mine said that one day I would write a book. I must confess, that having listened to many forecasts by other mediums, I dismissed this, for at that time the trance state had not developed, and I certainly had no thoughts of ever writing a book. This goes to show how wrong we can be-not that all mediumistic predictions come true. I'm sure that many of my medium friends would be the first to admit the fact that sometimes, the wires seem to get crossed,. Those who have read the first book, " Nobody wants to listen-and yet", will realise that some mediums can become aware of certain future events in our spiritual development.

The first book has been published and seems to be selling well. Since its publication we have continued to invite mediums to demonstrate in both Gibraltar and Spain. I have continued to listen carefully to the evidence given to my friends in the audience, yet still yearn to hear what I feel is irrefutable proof of life after death. Some of my medium friends have demonstrated psychometry as well as their gift of clairaudience or clairvoyance, and I question whether in some contacts they obtain their information by psychometrising the people to whom they give a message. In studying this, I am now convinced that objects have an aura that contains the history of their existence, so why shouldn't the auras of my friends provide a wealth of information that my medium friends can tap?

When Gordon Higginson came to Gibraltar, he gave two excellent demonstrations of his mediumship, and one lecture on the aura. During this lecture he told one lady that on that same day, she had bought an umbrella. Gordon told the lady the amount of money she gave the shopkeeper and also the amount of change she was given. Did he get this information from her aura or did one of his invisible friends whisper in his ear? Gordon said that the information was stored in the aura. It is told in Gordon's autobiography how, during one demonstration he gave a contact to a friend of mine-Carmen Antony. It is true that he described the interior of her daughter's house and even gave the address. Gordon also talked about a plant in the house, and about a Cameo broach which had belonged to Carmen's mother. I still question whether Gordon obtained this information from the aura, whether he psychometrised Carmen, or whether it was indeed information given to him by his 'Spirit helpers', guides or whatever name pleases the reader. I feel that a lot more research is necessary in the study of mediumship.

I still question what happens to me. Is it really Oliver and other friends transmitting thoughts into my mind, or is there another equally valid

7

explanation? Maybe some of the thoughts that I receive do come from invisible friends and mixed with some of my own subconscious knowledge and reading, provide a cocktail of verbal expression. Invisible friends continue to tell me that my doubt is my driving force-or am I telling myself? At least I try to be truthful. Maybe when I have finished this preface, some of the following chapters will throw a little light on this matter.

I was never aware of the thoughts that were given to me by Oliver and his friends, so that when I read the first book I could not believe that they had been transmitted through me. -I still say, "Why me? "Here we are trying to write the preface of the second book, without the slightest idea of what may follow in the ensuing chapters. My wife, who talks to the group nearly every morning, tells me that she has been told the titles of some of the chapters and that they are buried somewhere deep in my subconscious. Such a variety of topics were covered in that first book, that I sit here with apprehension wondering what may follow this preface. June does not tell me everything that my invisible friends tell her. Mary Duffy, one of the medium friends who visit Gibraltar forecast that another member of the group would make his presence known. Since Mary's visit, Charles Richet is now able to use me to express his thoughts. In earthly life he was a good friend of Oliver, and tells of the many experiments with mediums that they did together. He often speaks French then apologises to June, before continuing in English with a voice that resembles that of Maurice Chevalier. Although there was a little French in my education, he seems to have access to much more than I can remember. On the cassettes, I now hear Oliver, Phillippe, Charles, Sister Mary, Mentor, my father and my controller, Franz Anton Mesmer.

One of the thoughts expressed by Oliver Lodge and his friends in the first book was the fact that there was no such thing as coincidence, yet they also state that we have free will in both our and their world. I found it very difficult to reconcile these two ideas until I reflected on one or two incidents in my life.

When my wife and I visited London in order to try to publish the first book, a strange 'coincidence' occurred. As we made our way along the streets, my wife said,"look at all these book shops. Many of them seem to have old books in them. Perhaps you could ask if they have that book that Oliver wants you to read. "Here I should remind readers that in the first book Oliver said that he has been trying to influence my mind so that I would try to obtain a book written by his friend, Frederick Myers-the title being,"Human personality and its survival of bodily death". The assistant in the first shop told us that Myers' book had been out of print for a long time, but a man who was standing by my side, told us that a book fair was in

8

progress nearby in the Russel Hotel, and that when he attended the fair yesterday, he thought he saw the book that we mentioned. We hastened to the book fair, where a man kindly asked over a microphone whether any of the book representatives had the book that we wanted. Within a few minutes a small gentleman came towards us, holding a beautiful leather bound volume of "Human Personality and its survival of bodily death". Coincidence? ? I haven't yet had time to read it.

In 1980, a man was interested in buying our motor yacht and I said to my wife, "If the sale is successful I will devote the rest of my life to 'Spirit'". The sale was successful and off we went to America. On our return we saw that the same yacht had been arrested. The reasons are not important but eventually the yacht was auctioned. I suggested that we should attend the auction since we knew its value, and perhaps would be able to put in a bid for a price much lower than that for which we sold it. The auction was to take place in France necessitating crossing the English Channel. It blew a storm force ten. My wife June became so ill that I had to find a doctor when we landed. I bit into a piece of bread and one of my false teeth fell out. Eventually, we arrived in the port where the yacht was berthed, to find the yacht had been badly damaged in the course of its arrest. All the navigational equipment had been removed and the water and fuel tanks had been cut open. In our opinion the price of the highest bid exceeded its value so we abstained from even bidding. The moment we decided not to bid, everything seemed to go well. It seemed that a plane was waiting to take us back to Plymouth, where there was a connection to take us back to Gatwick. Many more incidents in this adventure reminded me that I had broken my promise by deciding to buy back that yacht. Everything went wrong when we were going, yet everything went right on our return. Coincidence?

Due to the fact that I have sat in trance on the radio several times here in Spain, and also in the offices of Psychic News, several reports appeared in that weekly newspaper. As a result of this, I have received many letters from people in different countries asking when the book is to be published. One of those letters came from a Mr. M. B. Radcliffe who had worked in Fleet Street, well known as the main publishing centre in England. A friend of his had sat with a medium through whom was transmitted the thoughts of Franz Anton Mesmer -now written in a book entitled "Magnetic Fluids and Planetary Influences". This happened at a time when I was in a quandary as to what decisions I should make with regards to publishing the first book. Was it coincidence that he read those articles in P. N. or was there a little intervention from my invisible friends? Oliver says that it is all part of a great plan. I could go on and on illustrating many other events in my life that on reflection would suggest that maybe Oliver and his friends were correct in that statement-There is no such thing as coincidence. I wonder whether in your life there are similar incidents that might help to emphasise this thought? ? One more 'coincidence'. Just before starting this second book my eldest son found he had no use for a word processor, so he suggested that I might be able to make greater use of it in writing any further books. I am using it at this very moment. Coincidence? ? I am not suggesting that every incident in our lives is a result of influence from the invisible world, for we have free will to either listen to them or ignore them. However, in my life it does seem that when I do heed their thoughts, my life runs smoother. Even this is a lesson.

Some friends of mine have recently returned from a trip to India where they witnessed the 'miracles', apports and teaching of that avatar Sai Baba. In the video that they kindly gave me, I heard Baba saying that although every religion may serve a purpose, he felt that universal love was the true way of life. Listening to the news every day, one is reminded that the bloodshed of yesteryear is still going on today-much of it in the name of religion. The world still seems to be plagued by war, violence, greed, selfishness, jealousy and other sins of society, yet we delude ourselves that we are civilised. My three dogs, two parrots and my favourite, the duck, seem to have more love in their nature than many humans. I'm sure that great light, 'Mentor', who sometimes transmits his thoughts through me, was correct when he suggested that the time has come for all religions to combine into one universal philosophy and that the prayers of all those religions should be replaced by spiritual contemplation. Forgive me for digressing,, but I feel sure that many readers feel just as ashamed of our human failings as I do

Returning to thoughts on Sai Baba and the phenomena which he often demonstrates, I am reminded of the healing and miracles that the Nazarene Jesus did and of the physical phenomena within Spiritualism. Also, often when I sit in trance, Oliver seems to have the ability to place his voice on a cassette even though it is held in my hands. Maybe the title of the first book "Nobody wants to listen-and yet", supplies the answer. If the Nazarene had not performed miracles, nobody would have listened to his spiritual teachings-the same with Sai Baba. Even the friends who visit us here seem more willing to listen to our invisible friends if some physical phenomenon is manifest. This is not a criticism-just an observation. I'm sure that I am the same as everyone else, yet it seems a shame that we all need something spectacular before we are really willing to listen to what our invisible friends have to say.

My wife, June has that wonderful gift of healing and I am privileged to witness many remarkable cures. In fact, if we were to send a report of the most spectacular results that have been achieved, it would make it appear that she is one of the most powerful healers of today. Instead, she prefers to feel those people who are meant to see her are guided to meet her. Sometimes friends only need to see her once in order to receive a positive result. Others come regularly, getting a little better each time. One lady who could hardly see, attended once a week for about a year. Now that lady has been given permission from her doctor to drive a motor car. During the year that she came for healing, I witnessed not only improvement in her eyesight, but also a change in her attitude to life, for not only did she receive healing energies, but the many conversations we had, made her aware of the reality of the invisible world. Although at that time the lady was taking the contraceptive pill, she became pregnant and now has a lovely baby boy. We are sure that this was also meant to be or the healing energies which flow through my wife can even overcome "The Pill".

Jane, who used to bring the lady with the bad eyesight, gradually took an interest in all branches of mediumship and now has developed a high standard of automatic writing. One day, June invited Jane to join her in what we call "table tilting". Half way through the session, Jane's right hand rose into the air and shook very very fast.. We felt that it was a sign of Spirit friends wanting to use her hand for the purpose of communication. Paper and pencil were put on the table and Jane began to write at a fantastic speed. At first it looked like scribble but we managed to decipher the word 'Welcome'.. Since that time it has developed to a standard whereby she is able to write communications given by friends in the invisible world, and give evidence of survival to the many people who visit us. Now the automatic writing is gradually giving way to clairaudience and clairvoyance.

Not everybody is healed in a physical sense. In fact some of our patients seem to have their time extended , but eventually leave earthly conditions, moving to one of those infinite levels of consciousness in the invisible world. We realise more than ever that even when this occurs, healing still takes place, for they are well prepared for their journey. Maybe only the healing successes of Jesus are reported in the bible. Those who were not meant to be healed are not mentioned. The same seems to apply when I use the tool of hypno-therapy. I remember a gentleman who had cancer of the liver, coming to see me. He said that he had heard that hypno-therapy could even help with such cases. This is true, for if we can assist a person to use the power of their own mind, I accept"Faith can move mountains". However, just as I was about to induce the necessary relaxation, a voice in my mind said, "You will not use hypnosis to try to help the physical, for this friend will leave your dimension in six earthly weeks. You will help

11

him prepare for that time". I obeyed the voice in my head and the gentleman passed exactly six weeks later.

Our Spirit friends have encouraged June to learn about reflexology, aromatherapy, acquapressure and the use of magnetism so that she may add these to that which is called 'Spiritual Healing'. It is interesting to watch how she seems to be inspired as to which tools of healing should be used with different patients. In his first book, Oliver Lodge mentioned the use of crystals in healing. He said that they were rather like an electrical condenser, in the fact that they could be charged up with healing energy, then discharged in to the person who needed the healing. These days, June also makes use of both colour and crystals in her healing-to great effect. I am not suggesting that all healers should follow in her footsteps for experience has taught me that all mediums, whether healers or clairvoyants work differently. Only by sharing knowledge and experience with one another do we learn.

My daughter is able to demonstrate flower sentience, although when I watch her work I feel sure that the flowers act as some sort of focus for mediumship. I remember on one occasion she seemed to be hold of what appeared to resemble a stalk with a golf ball stuck on the top. It was a flower but certainly didn't look like one. To the person to whom the flower belonged she said, "You used to keep chickens when you were younger", and a lot of other information which all proved to be correct. When I asked my daughter how she obtained the information, she simply said that whilst she looked at the flower, the thoughts came into her head. My mother used to give readings to people by looking at the tea leaves left in the cup. Others make use of a crystal ball, gaze into the fire or use tarot cards. A friend of ours has studied radio-onics and seems to be able to use it for the purpose of diagnosis. These days, there seems to be more and more branches of what is termed psychic. I feel that if they are used as a 'prop' for mediumship then all is well.

My eldest son, Philip is a physical medium in whose presence tables rise, trumpets move, sandals dance in the air and his Spirit friends communicate through his vocal cords. One of those friends says that his name is Sheaf-no, not chief. He says that he works on the sugar cane in Australia. I must confess that when he first said this, I wasn't aware that sugar cane grew in Australia. Philip is thirty eight years old and has recently got a new lady friend and naturally has not sat for quite a while, although the other day he did say that he felt the urge to sit again. I pray that he does, for although I have made comment about miracles and physical phenomenon, I must confess that I enjoyed sitting with him. The youngest son says that he prefers listening to Oliver and his friends.

As I mentioned earlier, my wife June has the gift of healing and the phenomenon of trance happens to me, yet even amongst such a spiritually gifted family my mind still searches for the ultimate proof of life after physical death. I wonder whether other mediums with their various gifts have similar feelings? Because June used to hear her name called when she was a young girl and the fact that she talks to my invisible friends daily, she is totally convinced of survival. She tells me that the voice she heard when she was young, was so clear, that she would turn round to see who was calling her, and as a result would often bump into another person or sometimes a lamp post. My trance state seems to convince many people that a group of discarnate minds use me to express their thoughts. I like to gather my evidence from listening to the many medium friends who we invite to demonstrate in the Gibraltar theatres. Often friends in the audience seem to receive excellent evidence, which convinces them of the survival of their loved ones, yet in the forty odd years of being involved in Spiritualism, other people seem to have got far better evidence than myself. Somehow, whatever happens to me, although convincing to others , I cannot count as evidence. A few people who knew Oliver Lodge verify the fact that his mannerisms and voice are the same as when they knew him. I admit that I am a 'Doubting Thomas'. That is probably the reason why I must enter an unconscious state before I can be used. My own father sometimes expresses his thoughts through me, but since I knew him when he was alive, I cannot except this as proof. At the same time, I cannot explain how he seems to know whether someone present has contemplated suicide, or knows of a suicidal friend.

A great interest is shown in reincarnation. We use hypnosis to help many to become aware of previous lives and whenever possible try to prove that the characters they claim to have been, actually did exist in the time of that incarnation. I must conclude from these experiments that either sixty per cent of all the people we see, have very excellent imagination or that there is some suggestive evidence for the fact that we have all lived many lives.What am I saying?If we have all lived many lives then there must be life after death.

An elderly lady lives in a house with a concrete floor in which appear faces. Our group have visited the house twice and verified that on the second visit there were different faces added to those there on the first visit. The house is in a small village, near Jean in Spain. When Mr. Albert Best saw the video of this happening, he became so concerned that he wanted to go to that village to help those poor souls who he felt had been in a limbo state since the days of the Spanish inquisition. Albert felt that only a medium could help them. If this is true, it seems a pity that most people who visit that place, do so with a sense of curiosity, rather than trying to understand the phenomenon.

Another lady who lives in Algerceras, is influenced to go to the beach where she finds stones in the shape of the organs and limbs of the human body. She places these stones in sea water, then when her patients place their hands in the water, it often turns blood-red. As a result of this phenomenon, by taking the stones home with them remarkable cures take place. I am surrounded by the gifts of my own family and all these strange mysteries, yet I still yearn for that absolute certainty of the survival of human personality after physical death. No doubt Oliver and his friends are smiling as I write these words. Let us see if he makes any comment when they express their thoughts after the preface. I used the expression"their thoughts", for it has already been said that in this book, there will not only be the thoughts of Oliver, but of the whole group.

One of the chapters in the first book was entitled"The kingdoms of life"After reading it I found myself encouraged to take a closer look at all the forms of life which surround me-the ants, lizards, birds, flies, our dogs, the duck, the parrots and much more. By the way, we did name one of the parrots after Oliver Lodge. We called it Ollie without being aware of the fact that one of Oliver's aunts wrote him a letter that started with' Dear Olly' 'Coincidence again! Television gives us a chance to study those forms of life that do not live in this part of the world. Now I can see better than ever, how mind takes the opportunity to evolve in all the different vehicles or bodies that evolution provides. Even as I write these words I can see hundreds of ants busy collecting food, and carrying more than their own weight to some underground nest. Their activities suggest a reasonable amount of intelligence, yet the size of their physical brain is minute compared with ours. If brain and mind are truly one and the same, then that of the ant makes the technology of our computers seem by comparison, inferior.

I give the dogs and the duck a cuddle every day and should I forget, sadness is expressed by their faces and eyes. Oliver said that those creatures who receive love from us do retain their individuality for a while, enabling them to meet us when we lay our mortal coil to one side. One of my invisible friends, Franz tells us of how his canary would come out of its cage and perch somewhere upon his person during his life on earth. After his death no-one could entice the canary out of its cage. Franz tells us that not long after his crossing to the other side, his canary joined him, retaining its individuality until there came a time when mutual telepathic understanding enabled the canary to put that individuality to one side, so that mind could move on to higher levels.

My friends in the 'spirit' world often remind us that they do not

14

have all the answers, and that often they can only express their opinion, therefore we are left with the difficult task of searching for that ultimate truth about birth, life and death. It is pleasant to see, listen and read of the experiences of others, but conviction of the survival of human personality is better obtained by personal and individual experiences.

Even as I try to write this preface, I feel a presence by my side reminding me that within Spiritualism there are Christian Spiritualists who place a greater emphasis on Jesus than those who belong to what is called "The Spiritualists National Union". Many in both camps accept reincarnation, whilst others prefer to believe we only live one physical life. In the same way, not all Roman Catholics adhere to exactly the same thoughts with regards to contraception and other controversial subjects. Surely, in truth, there are as many religions as there are people and those who are at the bottom of the scale in one, are very similar to those at the top of the scale in another, therefore we must conclude that each person is entitled to their views on these matters-without throwing stones at those who hold differing views. No doubt I will be put in my place when the preface is finished, and my invisible friends have the opportunity of expressing their thoughts on what I have said.

Often when I wake up in the morning, my wife tells me that one of the group have been talking to her, and that they would disagree with some of my thoughts or actions. They then give advice, but I, like many others often ignore it, only to find later that they were right-dead right. Oliver often quips with my wife telling her that he is both dead and right.

Although the first book contained mainly the thoughts of Oliver Lodge, there are seven invisible friends who manage to convey their thoughts through the medium of my mind. My wife tells me that even before they speak, she knows who it is because my face and posture change. At the end of the preface I will give a short summary, so that readers may know a little about the lives of each of my 'spirit' friends. The reason why Oliver Lodge took charge in the writing of that first book, was the fact that people still living knew him, and that to some extent my trance state could be put to the test-"Test the Spirit".

I had the pleasure of meeting Charles Stor, a gentleman who lives up the coast in Spain. When Charles was a boy he met Oliver Lodge and naturally wanted to hear Oliver speak through me. About one year ago Charles' passed over', but just before this happened, I received a request to go to Neja and sit for him. Oliver spoke to him for well over an hour, giving him great confidence in his last chapter of life and promised to be there to meet him when the final hour came. Experiences like these make me feel very privileged yet very humble. It reminds me that the greatest happiness is found in giving happiness to others-not in the gathering of personal treasures.

I, like my invisible friends can only express my opinion based on the experiences I have collected here in God's nursery school. It is never my intention to offend any individual or religion. If any reader feels upset by anything that I have written, let me apologise now. When I read the first book written by Oliver, I learnt a lot, enabling me to change my views on some Spiritual thoughts. Once again, I pray that as this preface closes, my invisible friends may so influence my mind and those of the readers, that we may together, have our minds stimulated by their greater knowledge and wisdom. By reading what they have to say, we may be able to draw a little closer to an understanding of the secrets and mysteries of God's creation.

The title of the first book was, "Nobody wants to listen-and yet". As I conclude, the title of this second book is already being whispered in my mind. It is-"For those who are willing to listen-READ-ON". FRIENDS

FRANZ

Franz Anton Mesmer, 1734-1815. An Austrian doctor, responsible for the term Mesmerer, 1734-1815. An Austrian doctor, responsible for the term Mesmerism, the forerunner of today's hypnosis. It could be said that he discovered animal magnetism, a branch of healing.

PHILLIPPE

Marquis of Puysegur, furthered Mesmer's work and probably the first to use hypnosis. He was president of the Paris Medicinal College. His proper name was Armand Marie Jacques Chasenet. He was a student of Mesmer and was probably the first to discover that hypnosis could be used in the psychic world.

Dr. CHARLES RICHET

Professor of physiology at the faculty of medicine in Paris-also president of the Institut Meta Psychique He did research with both Lodge and Myers and researched many physical mediums.

SISTER MARY

A nun in earthly life Now as part of the group she sometimes is able to give evidence of the survival to the people who attend our sittings. She is a medium in the invisible world.

HAROLD SMITH

My father, who seems to know if anyone present at sittings has contemplated suicide. He taught me how to build radios and many other things even though he was just a plumber. I feel that I respect him more now than when he lived on earth.

MENTOR

A wonderful soul, teacher to all others in the group. He is one of those souls who would say"What name do you wish me to give you", and seems to give a wealth of philosophy in every sentence. We feel that he dwells in a higher level of consciousness than others in the group.

OLIVER LODGE

A famous English scientist, pioneer of radio, the spark plug, and a host of other inventions which even benefit us today. His list of qualifications are too long to list and he prefers to be called just Oliver. In earthly life he was professor of physics at Liverpool university,principal of Birmingham university and devoted the latter part of his life to the investigation of mediumship, both mental and physical.

Sir Oliver Lodge

CHAPTER 1

"MAKE IT SO"

When writing books during my earthly sojourn, I often used the quotations of well known poets, professors or philosophers at the commencement of a chapter. In this book I intend to steal from the musical knowledge of Raymond, add a little of my own, and in simplicity use appropriate song titles to introduce various chapters. Greetings-

H ere we are again-Happy as can be
A ll good pals-and jolly good company"
F rom all those gathered with me here
O nce again we give truth to replace fear.
R aymond joins me to help with this rhyme,
T o bring peace from a sphere without any time.
H ere it is that inhibitions we lose,
O ur companions we are able to pick and choose.
S o every lesson in this world of the mind,
E nables us more and more answers to find.
W ith your patience and love we hope that you'll see
H ow happy one day you also will be.
O ut of darkness into light you will rise,
A nd find that to your great surprise,
R iches await you without any cost,
E mracements from those you thought you had lost.
W ar and aggression are things of the past.
I n there place is a peace that will last.
L ove is greater than you ever believed,
L ight is even brighter than your mind conceived.
N ow your companions are all of like mind.
G one are the pains of your earthly life,
T ogether with the tension, the stress and the strife.
O h what a joy You'll find it will be,
L iving in peace, great joy and harmony.
I ntelligent souls will help with their love,
S o you may realise they come from above
T o share with all that they possibly can,
E nhancing their knowledge of God's great plan.
N ow is the time for you to see,
R flections of what was and is to be.

E nlightenment comes to all who ask,
A nd you'll become aware of what is your task.
D oubt from your soul will be swept away,
O n a journey on which you'll forever say-
N ow I know that which I read was-TRUTH.

FOR THOSE WHO ARE WILLING TO LISTEN READ ON

In the first book that I was privileged to write through this medium, I explained how my son Raymond used to tell us of his whereabouts in acrostics and poems. I felt that it might be appropriate therefore, to start my contribution in similar manner-hence the title of this book expressed in the above simple poetic introduction.

From the butterfly world we fly back to the cabbage leaf from whence we came, alighting next to a caterpillar, hoping that we may once again be able to impinge our thoughts into its mind. I refer to this sensitive receiver Raymond, whose etheric brain pattern is nearly a simulation of that of Franz.

In the first chapter of the previous book I tried to transmit thoughts with regards to the difficulties of communication from our worlds to yours, but I feel that it was not sufficient. I would therefore like to transmit a few more waves on this matter, based on my experience gathered after 22nd August 1940-my rebirth. I use this term, for coming to the invisible world is in some ways similar to being born into the world of matter. Those who are willing to' read on' will reflect that at physical birth, they would only have vague memory of their entry into earthly conditions and hardly any memory of the time spent in mothers womb. It is rather exceptional for an infant to be able to remember from whence it came, yet the fact remains that a small number do. In similar fashion, entry into one of these levels of consciousness leaves one bereft of immediate memory of earthly conditions. Some who read these words may claim that they have received communication soon after the departure of some earthly friend or relative. If it was true communication, then I would suggest to you, that they were still relatively close to earthly conditions and had not fully entered what our teacher called the butterfly world. They had probably not even begun to spread their wings, ready for flight through the tunnel, into the light, and would only be able to convey limited thoughts-if any at all, as to the conditions in their deserved level of mind. Those who seem to return quickly, can only give reassurance of their continued survival, and even this is very difficult. Some who are knowledge-able of Spiritualism will know that I tried hard to convey the contents of the sealed envelopes which I had left with the S. P. R. I failed. It necessitates

20

much practice before one can transmit thoughts accurately and have those thoughts translated into appropriate words. I hope this will help to explain why many mediums seem to 'be in touch' with friends in our worlds, but often fail to give their names, addresses and other personal details.

My son Raymond first entered a level of mind, in which he said he could still enjoy a whisky and soda. He has moved on from that level and is now spiritually tee-total. Many who leave earthly conditions, linger in that tunnel of confusion for either a short or very long period of time-rather like an extension of dreaming. The time taken to pass into one of our 'many mansions', depends on many factors. Here one could draw a parallel with dreaming. Most dreams are relative to material matters-memories of yesterdays events, the present day, and hopes for the future, all relative to physical conditions. Even the dream world has an infinite number of levels, ranging from matters concerned with earth at the bottom of the tunnel, to entry into our worlds at the top of the dream tunnel experience. Like physical berth, only a few are able to remember 'from where they have come'. Those who are fortunate enough to pass quickly through that dream world with all its levels and into the light, are so dazzled by its brilliance that they cannot bring back full recollection of the experience they have just left. Even if they could, they would not want to return before exploring the new world in which they have just arrived.

Let us pause for a moment and consider the state of sleep and dreaming. Is it not true that in dreams, , one seems to be able to communicate with others without the use of language? If this statement be true, then the dream world is closer to our worlds than your limited conscious physical world. Is it not also true that often in dreams you are in the company of people whom you have never met in your present incarnation, and that your wife, husband and loved ones are temporarily forgotten? The dream world is that part of the mind world in which the fears, hopes and past memories of present and previous incarnations are expressed by the creative ability of the mind. It is also a condition in which those in our worlds, may more easily influence you-your mind, the real you. R. L. Stevenson deliberately used the dream world to acquire inspiration for his books. In fact, many great composers, inventors and artists were given inspiration whilst in a dream state, or an altered state of consciousness, that is often called day-dreaming. It is also true that loved ones can draw closer to you when you are in sleep state, and that often they form part of a dream. Let me assure you that when this occurs, it is not just fantasy but a condition in which you are closer to reality than when you are conscious and wide awake. I agree that there is a tendency to feel that earthly consciousness is more real than the unconscious sleep state or dream world. Whilst incarnate, the real mind world is constantly clouded by the physical and material. Mediums are able sometimes to sweep these clouds away, so that they may have a clearer view of the real world-the mind world , in which the cohesion of atomic particles is replaced by the union of parts of the personality-in which the etheric forces of gravity, magnetism and electricity on earth are replaced by higher etheric vibrations which determine the spiritual level to which you belong.

Dreams then can have a greater affect on you than your conscious daytime activities. Dream and sleep well. A few moments of sleep can give a regeneration, a different outlook on life, and can sometimes achieve what waking consciousness cannot.

What then will enable you to pass quickly through the confusion of rebirth and mature fast in the mind world? Only knowledge that the true purpose of earthly life is not the laying up for yourselves, 'Earthly treasures', but rather learning how to use experience to gain the wisdom necessary to navigate through the astral, etheric, , mental, spiritual and celestial worlds. The fact that many strange phenomena occur within three or four days of a persons death suggests that they are still close to earthly vibrations, and are able to manipulate certain energies that are in the lower etheric vibrations. Recently, I have been asked what I remembered first after my death. I related the fact that I was met by my friends Myers and Balfour, my sons, Raymond and Alex, brothers Richard and Alfred, my sister Eleanor as well as a host of other friends and relatives. I forgot to mention that I first passed through what I have called the dream tunnel and was in a confused state for a while. It was rather like recovering after an operation, when consciousness gradually returns as the anaesthetic wears off. In my gradual awakening, I recognised that those earthly friends and animals that I saw, had 'died years ago. The intellectual region of my mind quickly realised that I had joined them.

This medium reminds me in some ways of Myers, for he too could not bear to think that death was the end of everything. Here I must state that I stayed in a sleep condition for quite a few earthly days, rather like anaesthesia. It was only as I came out of this condition that I became aware of those who had come to welcome me home. Like a dream, time did not seem to exist and it would be difficult to say in earthly terms, how long that initial meeting lasted. Eventually, other higher minds took me to the level in which I now dwell. At this moment I am in one of the levels of the mind world, but can still put on the etheric counterpart of the body that I left behind. This is necessary for the purpose of working with this group in communicating to this medium.

When I have had the opportunity of linking with some groups of people still living on earth, some have accepted the fact that we all progress through the etheric, astral, mental and spiritual dimensions towards the celes-

22

tial. To where? What lies at the end of our journey?

It is gradually being accepted that space is infinite. Why then can not ones spiritual journey be infinite? We in our level of mind, can only try to describe the conditions in which we live. Trying to describe conditions in those levels that vibrate at a higher frequency, is a problem similar to your astronomists postulating the conditions that exist on other planets within galaxies that their instruments cannot reach. Neither can our minds see or the understand what lies beyond our mental and spiritual horizon, and find it difficult to give you accurate information with regards to that which we have not yet experienced.

Most mornings we take the opportunity of improving our ability to transmit thoughts to the mind of Raymond. This is necessary to maintain the degree of efficiency that is required in good mediumship. The concert pianist or violinist must practice daily for the same reason, yet there is a difference. In the case of the earthly musician the maximum performance is achieved when both mind and physical senses are in perfect union and harmony. In the case of good mediumship, it is necessary for the medium to be able to put aside the importance of those five physical senses so that finer sensing may take place. Until recently, it has been necessary for Franz to induce an altered state of consciousness, similar to sleep, otherwise Raymond would have analysed the thoughts received before verbalising them. Now we are able to telepathically transmit those thoughts without too much interference from the medium even in conscious state. This is a similar situation to that of Mrs. Piper who could work either in conscious state or deep trance. Practice makes perfect. The unconscious state gives us a better opportunity of including mannerisms, voice and other parts of our personality that would be harder to manifest during the waking condition of the medium. When in earthly life, I would often lie in bed and contemplate on the fact that I' was not in my foot, heart, liver, lungs, blood, or indeed any of the bodily organs. I must confess that when I considered my physical brain, I always entered the dream world before a conclusion could be reached. Religious superstitions of the past have suggested that the spirit did reside in certain parts of the body, and many of those superstitions still persist-some clinging to the fact that the Nazarene cast evil spirits into a herd of swine, whilst others feel that the spirit of an animal may affect them if they were to consume its blood. I would suggest to the intelligent, that the only consideration is whether brain and mind are one and the same. I now know that they are not, but since there may be some who want to listen-read on.

Today, many physical organs may be transplanted, yet the recipient of those organs still feels the same person. I admit that medical science has not reached that stage when the physical brain of one may be transplanted into another. The organs of the body are rather like the various components of the motor car, the engine being similar to the physical brain. In the mechanics of motor engineering one can change the engine as well as the components until all are worn out. The driver is not part of the motor car. He can decide to buy a new car or walk. More about a new body later-or doing without.

Man has made great strides to understand his environment and to govern his fate, yet seems to be afraid of tackling the important question as to whether he has a separate soul capable of surviving after physical death. Scientists have investigated the forces of nature, finding great truths, but have not yet found a way of solving the equation of man's destiny. This seems to have been put on the laboratory shelf labelled, "Religious superstition".

The only problem left then, is to differentiate between brain and mind. Even though some people are able to 'be out of their bodies', and verify that what they saw and experienced, maybe many miles away, did take place, this does not prove the persistence of mind after physical death. Only us who shave died know this to be true. How then may we prove this to you?

The idea of human survival has always been in the mind of man since he first evolved from those lower forms of life. This idea seems to be part of his natural instincts, and has been associated with most religions. In the science of the past, it has never taken root, but lately with the study of quantum mechanics, the possibility of parallel universes, infinite in number, it is gradually being accepted. At least this does fit with the statement, "In our fathers house are many mansions", and our conveyance of the fact that there are an infinite number of levels of consciousness. Religion and science are slowing converging, and only when they do join hands, will proof of that separate identity of brain and mind be found. In the meantime groups in our world will continue to try to bring about that unity. This will be more possible after the end of this millennium when much of the materialistic thought will be swept from the earth by a natural course of events. Can you not see that this has already begun? The increased prevalence of earthquakes, volcanoes, unrest, religious wars, intolerance , loss of purpose in life, are already obvious to the intelligent observer. Scientists may well eventually prove the existence of other universes by using very intricate and complex physical instruments, but they will only prove that intelligence exists in those universes by using non-physical instruments. The lower forces within the ether are only known by their effect on matter. We only know of electricity by its ability to produce light or heat, magnetism by its ability to repel or attract, gravity by the movement of stars and planets and the pull of earthly objects towards its centre. The higher forces within the ether may affect lower forces

24

and so mind through the ether may produce levitation, overcoming that lower force of gravity. Mind may also work through that ether to produce all sorts of physical phenomena, whether it be patterns in corn fields, objects in the sky, spirit photography, voices on magnetic tape or even pictures on your television screens. As long as you exist in matter, you may only become aware of any higher forces by their effect on matter. Proof of the separate existence of mind is very hard to achieve without the use of matter. At this moment I must work through that etheric counterpart of this medium to affect his physical vocal cords for speech, or his hand for what is called automatic writing. Great efforts are being made from our world to yours so that you may realise that there are some things that may not be explained by the laws of physical science, hence the necessity of that union between science and religion. This will only be achieved when religion throws away its false superstitions and science looks beyond what it can see in a microscope. If only there could be an intimacy between the mysteries within mother nature and father science, then would come the birth of an understanding of the true purpose of life on earth and death.

I agree with some of the statements made by Raymond in his preface with regards to communication, mediumship and psychometry. It is true that a vast amount of information may be obtained from the auras. Apart from differentiating between mind and brain, one must learn to also differentiate between sensitivity and true mediumship. Sensitives may receive information from the physical and lower mental auras of a person, and in their lack of knowledge feel that the information is coming from our worlds. Access to states of health, certain earthly memories and feelings are all there in the vibrations and colours of those lower auras. Only when information that cannot be stored within the aura of a person is given, can it be classed as mediumship. With Mrs. Piper and other great mediums of the past, proxy sittings took place when some other person would represent the one requiring the proof. The medium knew of this representation and yet was able to give to the proxy sitter information that could not possibly have been stored in their aura. In the same way, Mrs. Piper would often give me information with regards to the activities in the lives of some of my uncles. This information was not in my aura at the time. I had to often check it with other relatives. At the moment I feel you have many sensitives who can fulfil certain requirements, but not many mediums of the same calibre of those I and my friends were privileged to see in our life time. It does seem that the cloud of materialism has obscured the view and goal of good mediumship. From our observation through this channel, many people seem quite satisfied to be told what they want to be told, irrespective of whether it be true or not.

For the moment then we must accept that the spark of divinity within each one of you needs the vibrations of life force, mind and spirit before that spark can burst into a flame, then a light with sufficient intensity to make clear those mysteries and secrets of creation that have so far only been an allusion or a hope. Spirit needs mind, as mind needs ether to make some effect on the body, and that whilst manifesting in the world of matter, we need to see some physical manifestation to become aware of the existence of etheric, mental, spiritual or celestial vibrations. This means that those of you on earth need some medium' to use so that you may become aware of those other energies, just as light needs the ether and the reflection of its being on matter for you to see it with your physical eyes.

Mediumship in its many forms has existed since life blossomed into individualised mind. The butterfly has no doubt a very vague idea that it was not always a butterfly but finds it nearly impossible to communicate with those caterpillars it left behind. I am sure that most butterflies cannot remember being a caterpillar.

Applying this thought to communication from our world to yours, it must be remembered that"To one is given the word of wisdom, to another gift of healing" etc. etc. ". In this list is the discernment of spirit, a gift that enables some to be clairvoyant, clairaudient or clairsentient. The other gifts are in my opinion just as important , for not every clairvoyant is knowledgeable, wise, able to prophesy, speak in tongues or able to demonstrate some physical phenomenon. The list is constantly increasing for those in our world are aware of your advancements in technology. In my days it was not possible to place a voice on a magnetic tape for they did not exist. Not as many people were resuscitated from near physical death. Those that were, did not speak of it in fear of being ridiculed. Much more phenomena exists now, yet even the intelligent minds in both religion and science continue to look for alternative explanations as if trying to negate the possibility of communication from our worlds to yours.

I feel my friend Myers did prove telepathy, yet I agree it is as hard to find two people with telepathic rapport, as it is to find two snowflakes with the same crystal pattern. Occasionally there are two people whose physical and mental make up are sufficient to provide facilities for communication with each other, or from your world to ours. This type of communication is then very limited, otherwise it would not be necessary to seek and find. Snowflakes may have different patterns but if they were all melted by raising their physical vibrations they would all become water-able to mix together and in a sense communicate better. They would find it even easier if the vibrations were raised until the water became steam. Similarly, death puts aside the necessity of using physical means of communication, for the limitations of those patterns belonging to the body have gone-'dust to dust'.

The elemental vibrations change state. In other words the atoms of your body simply change their chemical structure just as paper turns to ash when you burn it. It has not disappeared since matter can neither be created nor destroyed, but either changes physical state or changes into radiative energy. I realise that those of scientific mind may want to remind me that radiation can eventually manifest as matter, by a change in energy vibrations, but nothing has been created or destroyed ; When the body dies, the vital returns to its appropriate level, as does those higher frequencies of mind and spirit. If only as much money and research were applied to telepathy and other non-physical forces as is in the pursuit of earthly pleasures, then science and religion would be able to become more intimate.

If your loved ones do not seem to communicate with you even through reliable mediums, do not think that they have forgotten you or gone for ever. The conditions in our levels of mind are so different than yours, that the dream parallel is the nearest that I can find to describe the situation. As I said earlier, it is rather like being born into the physical world, when it takes a time for the body to develop sufficient for the mind and spirit to express itself. Once mind becomes accustomed to its new surroundings, temporary amnesia disappears, memory returns, intellect is retained, scientific and artistic aptitudes continue and the love for those left behind often stimulates the desire to communicate. The difficulties of doing this are numerous as I mentioned in the first book. Invisible vibrations need some medium for you to become aware of their existence, just as magnetism needs iron filings for you to know of its presence. Sensitivity may be the training ground for mediumship but by itself it is not sufficient to provide the necessary link from our worlds to yours. The magnetism does not affect the filings directly but only through the ether that pervades within and around them. We need some mind capable of responding to the transmission of our thoughts, so that you may know of our presence. Even then, the recipient mind must work through the ether to produce some physical reaction, whether it be speech, writing or some other phenomena which appeals to those five senses. Unlike my friend William Crookes. I never had the opportunity of witnessing full materialisation, but in his chateau of Carqueiranne, Richet, through the mediumship of Eusapia Palladino convinced me of the reality of levitation and telekinesis, forces not easily explained by science alone.

I am aware that there are some incarnate minds who feel that proof will be found in mathematics and science. Most religions feel that blind faith is sufficient. Only when religions put away the tool of fear and use the tools of science will the knowledge of survival be substantiated.

When in earthly life, I often thought that there was no point to living if all was lost at physical death. Now we know that all is retained and that opportunities of adding to what we are already, are limitless. Even though the opportunities of good communication are rare, we are able to often influence your minds without you even being aware of it. Not every thought that enters your mind has its origin in yourself. Many of those thoughts come from the guidance of those who know of your spiritual needs more than yourself.

How many dots of a pencil can you put on a line three inches long? It obviously depends on the size of each dot. Imagine that you could make each dot smaller and smaller then you could put an infinite number of dots on that line-or could you? It would be rather like splitting the atom, for eventually the dot could not exist in matter form, but would change into etheric vibrations or sub-atomic particles instead of physical atoms of matter. I emphasise once again that as your bodily particles of matter degenerate, the finer particles still persist, although now not visible to the human physical eye-only visible to those who are sensitive enough or developed to use the eyes belonging to their non-physical other bodies. Those who are capable of using the etheric eyes may behold the etheric body and colours of others. Those who have developed sufficiently to use the mental eyes can become aware of other minds. In the same way spiritual eyes can see not only the mind, but the spiritual vibrations of others, whether incarnate or discarnate. Since none of us have even started to vibrate the celestial part of us, we can not (see) comprehend God.

The wife of this medium and I were discussing the infinity of space, and she like many, finds it reasonable to accept that providing there are no 'heavenly bodies' in the way, space is possibly infinite. In the same way she can accept that progression of mind and spirit is also infinite, but wanted to know where we all started. I tried hard to stretch her mind to accept that if there is no end to spiritual development then there was no beginning. Infinity stretches in both, or should I say infinite directions. The essence of my being has always existed even though once its particles (sub-sub-sub, etc. , atomic) were probably in a state of staticsticity-not started to vibrate.

Communication from our world to yours reminds me of the experiments done in extra sensory perception, using zener cards. Those of you who have tried these experiments will know that even a score of thirty per cent suggests mind is capable of influencing other minds. This score is exceptional and accounts for the fact that there are not many mediums capable of exceeding it, especially when they are in conscious state. In my world communication with one another is of course by thought which has many facilities, for it contains emotion, visual transmission of images (clairvoyance) and transmission of feelings (clairsentience). Thought embraces the use of music and all other forms of art. Language is no longer necessary. On earth, you have to use some means of transport to get from one place to another. Here a thought is sufficient. It is not limited by the speed of radio waves. If there is a common desire for people to be together in a certain place, it occurs, with the willingness of those in a higher level to lower their mind frequency, enabling them to instantly join their friends who dwell in lower levels. In university, those in their fourth year may visit friends who are in their first year without having to stay there. Whilst there,they may be able to help first year students with certain problems. First year students may be invited to witness the activities of fourth year students, but would find it difficult to understand everything they saw.

Mind is the governing factor. Some religions suggest that after death, one must wait for the day of the great resurrection. Others would say that only a certain number may enter the kingdom of heaven. It is said by others that if mind has not evolved sufficiently, the spirit would enter the body of an animal or some other form of life. With regards to that near death experience, I have already stated that the biblical figure some claim to see, is really their 'spirit guardian', taking on the guise of what the mind expects to see. What then happens to the mind that expects resuscitation on that day of resurrection or the minds of those with other expectations? This is the reason why some would stay in that dream-like, confused condition until it is felt that they are ready to accept greater truths. All religions with their various beliefs exist in our world. Many states of mind exist in-between the sleep of death and re-birth into the reality of one of those' many mansions'

Every religion feels that it holds the truth. Some accept reincarnation—others do not. Does God really want the leaders of these religions to decorate their churches with gold or does God prefer a meeting place to be simple? Here I must stress the fact that God is the name we give for infinite intelligence.

Is it necessary for ecclesiastics to dress in elaborate robes or would it be better to dress simply as some of the past great teachers did? Does every cleric really believe in that which he or she teaches or for some, is it just a profession? Is every spiritualist medium spiritual, or do some use their gift for personal gain? Whether priest, vicar, rabbi guru, or medium every person is surrounded by invisible friends of similar mind. Birds of a feather flock together. Is it important whether one of these mediums or priests smokes or drinks or is it more important that they use their talent, knowledge, wisdom or gift for the welfare of others? Those of us who manage to find a person receptive to our thoughts, have to use that medium irrespective of whether they are spiritually minded or not. It is better if they are.

As I said in the previous book, those who receive communication from our world, do so from its infinite levels, in which the knowledge, experience, wisdom and spirituality differ. It is no wonder then that the true answers to all these questions is hard to find. We do not pretend to have those answers or to know the secrets of creation. All that we may share with you is the condition that prevails in our level and the evidence that we have survived.

It must be said that not all those who belong to one of those orthodox religions accept all its teachings. This is well illustrated when Raymond invites mediums to demonstrate their gifts in some large theatre. I understand that although most of those who attend are Roman Catholics, they hope to receive communication from a loved one who dwells in one of our mind worlds. They obviously do not accept that after death they have to wait for the day of resurrection. Whatever their mind truly believes will determine the time taken to pass through the dream world into their particular level. Only those who really believe they have to wait, will wait until they can be awakened from their self induced coma. As I have said previously, there are as many beliefs as there are people, and therefore that is the reason why the time of awakening is different for each soul. What about the atheist who does not believe in God or the agnostic who only accepts that which is material? I'm sure that you have heard that some souls do not accept that they have died and naturally stay in the lower section of that dream world tunnel, close to earthly conditions. Rescue circles like those organised by my friend Hugh Dowding, try to help these poor souls realise that they have died and that they must travel towards the light. No wonder then that conditions prevail where faces appear in the floor, as this medium reported in his preface. In making these statements, I am speaking of the true agnostic or atheist, for many who claim to be one of these, secretly hope that they are wrong

Science generally relies on observation and repeated experimentation before it can accept a theory based upon the facts gathered. The production of hydrogen and oxygen may be achieved by anyone who places two cathodes in water. Religious beliefs are based upon the testimony of those who witnessed phenomena outside the laws of science. Often these phenomena cannot be repeated at will, making scientists sceptical about their reality. Members of the Royal Society were invited to witness some of the experiments that my friend Crookes did with the medium Home, but they refused saying that the results were mechanically impossible. Had they witnessed those experiments they would have demanded that they were repeated under their conditions. We cannot guarantee to place this medium in an unconscious trance condition every time, nor can we place a voice on a magnetic tape every time he sits. It depends upon the conditions that prevail each time. Those conditions lie outside the realms of physics and chemistry. So it is that science, religion and communication still have little in common. As I said earlier, I urge men of science to put away their microscopes for a few moments so that they may realise those parallel universes are inhabited by intelligences of infinite levels—that sub, sub, sub atomic particles could be the substance of the invisible world. A time approaches when the forces of nature will make them realise that they are no longer the Gods of the material world and that the laws within both science and nature belong to an infinite intelligence that cannot be verified by science or religion alone, but only by their co-operation.

Communication from our worlds to earth has taken place ever since man gained his individuality. Unfortunately this communication has been ignored by science and relegated to the superstitions of religion. " They cannot see the wood for the trees" , is a favourite saying used by the father of this medium. So much strange phenomena exists yet instead of trying to understand its origin, mankind seems to prefer to ignore it. Scientists accepted the existence of thunder and lightening but refused to study it until Franklin proved it was of an electrical nature and was therefore subject to repeated experiment and measurement. Religion in the past made it a God.

Physical death is inevitable. Do not ignore it. Experiment with all the various forms of communication from our world to yours. Use the tools of science together with the faith of religion to prove the immortality of the soul. When this is accepted as a fact, the scourges of war, jealousy, greed and materialism will be replaced by a nirvana of peace, sharing, kindness and above all-love. If there were many means of reliable communication from our world to yours, surely all of those with an interest in the welfare and love of those left on earth would take every opportunity to shout " We still live" We cannot shout, but have to rely on telepathic means of communication. Telepathy relies on visions, on sounds, on feelings, on emotions, mannerisms of personality but not on any specific language. This is well illustrated by the other kingdoms of life who often seem to understand man and one another without the use of a common language. Dolphins often feel the cry for help from human friends and have been known many times to respond to that cry, saving many a life. So it is here. We try to transmit our thoughts in many ways and jump for joy if the receptionist or medium is able to sometimes express our thought in an appropriate word or even name. The physical body may be likened to a lead shield through which it is very difficult to transmit radio waves. Once that shield is removed, reception is easy. In the higher regions of the invisible world the limitations of physical energies no longer inhibit the exchange of thought, just as in the higher regions of the dream world thoughts seem to be shared without the use of language. 'For those who are still willing to listen-`-Read on'-as other friends add their thoughts to mine. I will join you later.

Mentor (The Teacher)

CHAPTER 2

"I BELIEVE"

Good morning. My name is not important. Neither is the knowledge as to in which country I last incarnated. I have no need to adorn my body with either ecclesiastic robes or even a simple garment. It is true that in travelling through lower levels of mind, I may take on the etheric garments belonging to any of the incarnations still within my memory. Every mind is a part of God. If I choose to wear the robes of a priest, or a simple garment, it is not the garment that is important, but the mind's motive in wearing it. There are possibly as many motives as there are priests. Let us not judge by what we see, hear, touch, smell and taste, for these senses are limited. How may we judge others when we do not even understand ourselves?

It is always an honour to be able to share my thoughts with you for as you allow those thoughts to blend with yours, you give me and my friends the opportunity of trying to be of service-thus enabling us to move a little further along a never ending pathway, an infinite adventure on which I pray my light may shine a little brighter with each step that I take. Your spirit friends know of both your needs and wants. As Oliver has already stated-these two are often different. Your thoughts are the prayers that we hear. Earthly children are full of wants but the wise parent would attend to their needs. To do this well, they must use discipline, then direct them through life's necessary experiences. By doing this they show greater love than if they gave their children what they wanted. Know then that your spirit friends show their love and guidance by attending to your needs rather than your wants

My friend Oliver has talked of infinite levels of consciousness within those mind spheres attached to your planet, yet often he would confine his thoughts to the human species. May I take this opportunity of reminding Oliver and his group that infinite levels of mind exist in all other forms of life not only on your planet but within God's ever expanding creation. Not only does the human species have different colours of skin.. Differences are seen in the fingerprints, the lines on the hands and other bodily features in all forms of life, and since births take place every second, these features are for ever increasing-infinitely! Even the ant to which Oliver often refers, seems to have a reasonable level of intelligence and displays a sense of communal responsibility; I suggest that it may, in some ways be less selfish than mankind. If time is taken to observe it's life, even that level of mind called reasoning can be seen. Some of these creatures

33

bury their dead friends. In the animal world it can also be seen that some have greater loyalty, intelligence, reasoning and even emotion than others. Without enumerating every kingdom of life, I urge you to reflect on the fact that infinite levels of mind apply not only to mankind, but in every manifestation of life on your spec of dust, planet earth. as well as in other parts of God's creation. The length of stay in earthly conditions varies according to the form of life, ranging from less than one day for an insect mind to hundreds of years as shown by a tree. Ornithologists may put a number to the variety within the bird world, yet every eagle has a different personality and eagles are being born constantly. As one form of life becomes extinct another vehicle of mind is created. My friends have stated that every snow flake has a different crystal pattern. It has been snowing somewhere ever since earth cooled sufficient to allow this process. Mind whether in animate or inanimate form takes the opportunity of expressing itself in an infinite number of ways, for even in the mineral kingdom, one can observe different properties in every type of rock. Is the law and order of this kingdom always confined to that mineral world, or does it have the opportunity to expand until it passes from inanimate to animate then from one form of life to a higher one?

Who then is the architect, artist and scientist that is responsible for these infinite varieties of expression of mind. God? Who or what is God?

Mankind in his lack of understanding of infinity, feels that God made man' in his own image'. No doubt the dog feels that mankind is its God. I wonder what the ant envisages as God? That infinite space must present life with infinite ways of manifestation and each life form must have a different conception of God no matter in which part of creation it exists.

With regards to all the opposing views in science, religion and those expressed in communication. I suggest that those who refuse to listen to the others point of view may be afraid of learning the truth-the fact that no incarnate or discarnate mind knows God's truth. Life is an infinite process of learning. Birth, life and death are simply different classes in an infinite school of learning. The mind is like that infinite space, so why do you limit it? In the discovery of greater truths it throws out the old to make room for the new. Young souls think that they know everything. Old souls realise that they hardly know anything. The young are full of wants. Old and wiser people realise that the only lasting thing is love, a quality desired in every kingdom of life. Love becomes finer with every step taken on your spiritual journey.

If your loved ones and friends who have joined our dimensions could make you hear the two words expressed by their minds, those two words would be, "If only". "If only I had known that all forms of life had

34

souls I would have fed the birds. If only I had known that I was going to die when I was thirty five years old, I would have shown my love for you more than I did. If only I had known that my friend needed more help, I would have given it. If only I had known that my son would squander my hard earned money, I would have travelled more and given more to those in need. If only I had been able to replace faith and hope by knowledge The list is endless. If only they had been sure of the reality of life after death, then they would not have put as much emphasis on the material and physical aspects of life. Take your eyes away from earthly conditions and see that there are abundant mysteries that can only be explained by the acceptance of energies with vibrations much higher than any on earth.

Use the intelligent level within your mind and imagine that you had command over every means of transport: that you could travel however you wished to any part of your planet. Imagine also that you had power over every other person and that you had an unlimited, nay, an infinite supply of money. In that imaginative level of the mind, imagine also that other peoples friendship and love were subject to your command. Imagine also that you could live in these earthly conditions for ever. Do you really feel that in this earthly utopia you would find happiness? Those of you who answer "Yes" , will return to this fictitious utopia over and over again until you eventually realise that no earthly condition will provide the happiness you seek. Only by learning that earth is truly a nursery school in which it is necessary to learn that giving is as joyful as receiving, that in order to receive love, one must give love. There is much more joy sharing what you have with others, rather than keeping it for oneself. The books of religion may have been infected by the thoughts of the ecclesiastics of old, yet they still contain treasures of philosophy. The treasures of the spirit do not die. The memory of the old lady that you helped will live longer than the memory of any material object that you possessed. The memory of having shared knowledge instead of selling it, is a more lasting memory. 'Lay not up for yourselves treasures on earth, but rather treasures of the mind'

The earthly musician needs an earthly instrument upon which to play. He or she would sometimes need the music written by the mind of others or the ability to create a melody within their own mind. Either way, the sound of the music depends on the expressive ability of the player's mind. Similarly, in communication from our world to yours, we need a good earthly instrument who has the mental capacity to be able to express our thoughts in some way that appeals to the physical senses of others.

Some earthly minds have the ability to move physical objects, because they can exude from their body an energy capable of doing this. They may allow this energy to be used by discarnate minds and therefore do not presume that all physical phenomena is the result of discarnate minds. Levitation is not always due to " The Spirit World". Wonderful music may be composed by both incarnate and discarnate mind even though an earthly hand must write it. Not every scientific thought or invention is a result of an earthly mind. Thought from our worlds have then infinite ways of expression. Doctors and nurses are often influenced by invisible friends who still take an interest in the welfare of the body. " To one is given the gift of healing". Artists often receive inspiration from those who want to help in that particular form of expression. Earthly interests are maintained for a while in our world and the inhabitants find that they can find joy in being of service to those left on earth by inspiring them to achieve greater results than they did. Whatever be your interest, be assured that invisible friends gather around you trying to add to your thoughts-if you are willing to listen. We in the invisible world have laws that only permit us to give help to those who are incapable of helping themselves. In reading these words you may feel that certain parts of your world are in dire need of help. Are the people in that part of the world truly not capable of helping themselves? High intelligences, on God's behalf constantly present mankind with mysteries to solve as part of the learning process. It would not be common sense if invisible friends, like the group here, were to provide all the answers. They do not know all the answers. Different mysteries are presented in every sphere, in every level within those spheres making that learning process infinite.

On earth, mankind is aware of his physical existence and the laws that govern it. Only a few can remember from whence they came. The inhabitants of the etheric world know of etheric conditions and only a few find the opportunity to remember in great detail the full memory of their time spent in earth's prison. Just as man has put aside memories of the evolution of his mind through the mineral, vegetable and animal kingdoms, so those in the mental, spiritual and celestial spheres have put aside unnecessary memories of their passage through earthly levels. Mankind always retains the benefit of all previous experience. Those in etheric and mental worlds often have to express their thoughts in symbolic terms in transmitting guiding thoughts to those in their charge. I pray that this explains why Myers, Oliver's friend was only able to communicate through a medium in literary fashion instead of actual words. When a voice of one of the group manifests on a magnetic tape it is not their voice, but the result of the physical energy provided by this medium and the words interpreted from a transmitted thought. Even in the physical phenomenon of direct voice, the thought reaches the mind of the medium who then passes that thought through the ectoplasmic cord attached to the voice box. The words that you hear are only a telepathic transformation of that thought. Generally, those in earthly conditions have to rely on some language to convey thoughts to one another. Those in our worlds use the language of mind to communicate with each other. Is it not true, as Oliver said, that in the dream world, you seem to be able to communicate without having to use your voice, yet those with whom you communicate understand better than if you had used words.

At this moment I rely on the transmission of pictures, feelings, emotions and guidance of this medium into appropriate situations, praying that these may result in a true transcription of my thoughts. Only occasionally by the transmission of sound can we hope that he receives an actual word. A baby is aware of its mothers feelings long before it has the ability to speak. An animal and even a plant will respond to the emotions of mankind. I avoid using, the term man, for mind and spirit have no sexual gender. As Oliver would say-male and female are two necessities in the development of mind. After the etheric, astral and mental spheres all are the same in the sense that there is no need for sexual gender. Evolved Spirit is the result of all lessons learnt during the male and female incarnations. The soul does not any longer need the lessons provided by manifestation as male or female.

Since mankind is only sure of his existence in body form, he doubts whether survival is possible without a body. Those in etheric wavelengths wonder whether it is possible to survive without the etheric body, for that is their world at that time. I assure you that the inhabitants of the mental levels wonder whether mind will persist for eternity. The spiritual sphere with all its levels is beyond our conception. How then can any of us hope to understand that which we call God? In whichever sphere we are privileged to dwell we can only say, " I am". My friends here suggest to you that even in the smallest part of matter, law and order can be observed, even though in primitive form. It can be seen that it expands as life force makes use of matter. Is human manifestation the highest limit that mind can reach? Two of Oliver's sons join me, wanting to help express my thoughts in rhyme. It is my pleasure to welcome them.

What is this life all about
All I can hear is people shout
Oh for a little peace in my life,
To take me away from trouble and strife.
This world seems full of jealousy and greed
On money and power does mankind seem to feed.
Loving thy neighbour is a thing of the past,
Because all in life really moves too fast.
There's more to life than the eye can behold.

No-one seems the truth to have told.
Stop for a while and look at the stars.
Come out from behind life's prison bars.
Now you might see that space has no end.
You might even hear the thoughts that we send,
Telling that death is nothing to fear.
All your loved ones are so very near.
So look much further than your eye can see,
Then from that prison you then will be free.
You'll then know that life is well worth while,
Enabling you to for ever smile,
Knowing that life goes on for ever.
Love is the one thing nothing can sever.
The beginning of all things seems to be blurred
When life force first this planet disturbed
Mind then entered to add its vibrations
Creating the seas, land, life, even nations,
Part of this plan involved husband and wife
Knowing learning involved much stress and strife,
Male and female were just part of the scheme
Duality in all things added to life's dream
That one day we would reach that very high sphere
Where no longer existed any state of fear.
The challenges set us have now been won
Our work there we have now finally done
Now we can return to that home above
To reap more the blessings of God's love.

Oliver's sons encourage you to look at life; not just your own but
life as it exists in so many forms. Science admits that it cannot explain it.
Religion prefers to attribute it to some personified being. We are in the
same wilderness, in the fact that our minds have not evolved sufficiently to
understand the infinity of creation. Let us blend our thoughts, using the
intelligent level of mind to see that everything that exists had some cause.
We are just one of the effects. I am here because I came from the etheric
world. Those who inhabit that world came from the world of matter. From
whence came the matter world. According to Oliver and his fellow scientists earth in its solar system came from the sun. The sun is but one of an
infinite system of radiations. Who started that radiation. A big bang? Who
lit the fuse? God is the infinite cause. Science and nature together—the infinite effect.

Those who I am privileged to hear would say that there is no such thing as evil-that which is termed evil is the epitome of ignorance. How then can we all help to rid our worlds of ignorance? You in your world can teach by using the facility of words, but as Oliver would say" Nobody wants to listen-and yet". And yet there is a finer way of teaching-that of setting example to others. If you put great emphasis on material and physical aspects of life, do not be surprised if your children and friends behave in similar manner. Everyone who manifests in body form has come back to earth's school, knowing that in that school certain lessons must be learnt. Some of those lessons may only be learnt in female form whilst others are learnt in male incarnation. This is just one example of the duality that provides you with nearly infinite experiences on earth. The mind needs to gather enough strength to retain its deserved individuality. This strength can only be found by incarnations as both male and female, by being rich and poor, beautiful and ugly, strong and weak, positive and negative, healthy and infirm. The list is infinite. Because of this, can you not see that one incarnation in human form provides a very limited number of these experiences? The lower forms of mind have the opportunity to incarnate with a different vehicle of manifestation. Having reached human level it has only just been awarded that certificate of individuality. Mankind's mind has reached a spiritual viscosity to enable it to stay as a droplet of mind rather than have to join a sea of mind,as lower forms of life do. Since no more advanced vehicle than the human body is available on earth, the mind must return until it has mastered every challenge that human life provides. Only then is it fit to face greater challenges in those worlds made of higher vibratory substance than matter. As I transmit these thoughts I realise that many cannot except the concept of reincarnation. May I repeat the fact-it is not what your mind can except or want, but rather what your mind needs.

I urge you then to have as many experiences of great variety in your earthly lives, to realise that the extremes of every situation provide an opportunity of learning. If you really develop a great empathy for the deaf, dumb and blind, then you need not experience those conditions. If, whilst you are rich you use those riches to help the poor, you need not incarnate in poor conditions. Whatever be your circumstance in earthly life, try to fully appreciate those who dwell in opposite or other conditions. Scientists should appreciate all forms of art. Artists must learn to appreciate the wonders of science.

In all of life's challenges, the attitude of mind is of the utmost importance. The same activity that is called work by some, others may treat as play. I too can use the treasures of the mind of this medium and find there a story. The boy who plays on the sand with his bucket and spade is happy doing that activity without any reward. He is playing. Only a short distance away, the man who has to load his cart with sand, then empty it, does it for some financial reward. He is working. Take joy in painting your house, in painting your neighbours house, in every activity that life provides. Stress and tension will no longer be able to reside in your mind, and therefore will not manifest in your body. Cast not only your bread upon the water, but the whole of your life, and life will return to you not only a hundred fold but for eternity-infinitely. God is love. You will only find love by giving it-not for reward, but for the joy of giving. Oliver's science teaches that matter may neither be created nor destroyed. That science has yet to learn that mind also cannot be created or destroyed. It has always been and will always be. God is infinite love. We are all on an infinite journey in search of God.

I am aware that many would consult mediums wanting to know what lies in their future. The true medium is a link between our worlds and yours. We are not able to interfere with your free will and can only relay thoughts from your friends in our world, who do not know what decisions you are likely to make. Matters concerned with earthly life are often shown by the colours and energies in your aura. Psychics and sensitives can often become aware of that which lies below the conscious mind, helping you to discover your hidden passions and therefore the best pathway to tread.

Look at a new born baby. The body may be new but the soul is not. Is it not common sense that it must temporary forget from whence it came? Memory of the level of mind that it left would take away the very purpose of another life. The few who do remember often turn faint hearted, return from whence they came and try again later. Friends join me once again so that I too may conclude my contribution with a poem. Poetry, music, sculpture and other forms of art can often express thoughts better than words.

MY PRAYER FOR YOU

May I and my friends each and every day
Try to help you find your way
Out of darkness into the light
There against ignorance more able to fight
Let us all by our every deed
See to that which our friends really need
Taking from them sorrow and pain
So that they may find love again
They know there's always by their side

One who tries their life to guide
We can hear your every plea
And try from tears to set you free
Those you have lost still for you care
And want in your life still to share
They have learnt it's good to be kind
To all they feel they've left behind
It's only the body that they have shed
Do not to others say they're dead
Know although they now dwell above
They are much closer to God's love.

Do not be like many of your friends who on returning to the real
world have said,"If only", but know now that earthly life is a trial—a test-
ing of whether you have gained sufficient wisdom to gain freedom from the
chains of the prison called earth. Replace your faith and hope by the knowledge which your spiritual friends try to transmit. I thank you for listening to
my words and now stand to one side whilst others try to be of service. In
my lack of ability to give a clearer definition of God than infinite intelligence
     May God Bless You.

Franz Anton Mesmer

CHAPTER 3

"IF I HAD MY WAY"

Ich kann nur gebrochen Englisch. Guten Tag. Good day. I express my thoughts relying on Raymond to receive them well and express them in his language. Yes, I am Franz Anton Mesmer and it is I who found that this person could react to my every thought. I am not his guide, but his close friend in the group that assembles here. The term guide is an earthly word that many have copied and imitated since the birth of spiritualism. He is my earthly friend. Many earthly years ago, when this medium was quite young, he took a great interest in the power of the mind and of energies outside the realms of earthly sciences. My friends here have told you that in our worlds, the only punishment is that which you inflict upon yourself as a retribution in an attempt to rectify mistakes made whilst in the body. I admit that in my earthly work , I allowed success to be more important than the actual curing of my patients. In his early days this medium also fell into the same trap. Because of his inner desire to use what is termed hypnosis for the good and because of our telepathic rapport, I take the opportunity of using him to pay both his and my debts.

In both mine and your days it must be realised that it is possible for one man to address thousands of people and in so doing affect a whole nation as a direct result of suggestion, the base of your modern hypnosis. Men like Karl Marx, Hitler and others in positions of political or religious authority have amply demonstrated this and still do today. What is called hypnosis, like all good things can be abused, and is by the extravagant claims of stage and amateur performers. Hypnotism is not a substitute for religion or science but it may, if used properly, enable you to find that power within you-the kingdom of God. Oliver has given his thoughts on healing. " Physician-heal thyself" , if interpreted properly means that the doctor should not only be able to advise his patients on the correct use of herbs, or in modern days-drugs, but also be able to help people cure themselves. Apart from the germs and viruses that invade our bodies, to help strengthen the immune system, the mind is the greatest healer of all. The bible abounds with instances of healing and I feel no irreverence in suggesting that Jesus and other great teachers helped people to use the power of their own minds to show the miracles of healing that are reported. By using it for themselves, martyrs have been able to withstand terrible torture without feeling any pain. It has been used for centuries in Eastern countries by holy men to develop super-normal powers. It is my opinion that if a person had sufficient faith in the Turin shroud a miracle cure could be effected. The same cure would take place if an imitation shroud were used. In the past, kings have cured many by giving what was called' The Royal Touch'. This I know to be the origin of the laying on of hands. I do not disagree with Oliver's comments on the flow of vital energy from the healer to patient, for this is what I described as a 'magnetic fluid'. This energy may be given by the healer from the aura and added to by invisible friends, who have the ability to transmit telepathically energies from our dimensions. The energy which I said came from the stars, filling the whole universe, is the same energy that you today call cosmic energy and this energy exists in various frequencies in those infinite levels of consciousness. It is this energy that spirit friends transmit telepathically to the healer , thence to the patient.

I feel it very important to stress that any patient can either open their mental door to the energies of healing or close that door. As I mentioned earlier, all the great healers of the past had their failures- not due to their fault but rather the doubt of the patient. This doubt can equally apply to the world of medical practice for I have known people to recover and die from the same operation and suggest that their mind was the controlling factor.

A person may grow red in the face because of embarrassment. Another breaks into a cold sweat because of fear. Some tremble. Without giving further examples those who have, 'read on' wil ealise that many physical symptoms have their origin in the mind- not the brain. Many think that hypnosis involves the necessity of entering a deep sleep state. Nonsense. One of the biggest vampires of your minds are the thoughts given to you by your modern systems of communication-your radios, televisions and newspapers. Those in charge of these systems are either religiously or politically biased and a vast majority of mankind allow themselves to be thus influenced. How many of you have taken the trouble to study politics and religion? " Be true unto thyself". Have you allowed yourself to be misguided by your parents, other relations or even friends? The behaviour of these people may affect your whole life, for often actions are more suggestive than words. Why look down on lower forms of life when often you yourselves behave as sheep, following one who has lost its way. If I had allowed my parents to dominate my life I would have been a minister of some church. So would Oliver, Raymond and others in my group.

Oliver has already informed you that his interest in these matters started when he witnessed 'mind reading', by some girls in some drapery stores. Armand continued my work and extended it to discover the power of suggestion. Charles, also is enthusiastic about using the mind for healing. In fact the whole group assembled here have gathered together to try to convince you that you are your mind, and since it persists after physical death, it would seem common sense to pay more attention to its development than even that of your temporary physical body. In an effort then to make good my mistakes of the past, I would like to take this opportunity of explaining how I would work if I still had my physical body.

There are seven spheres of mind existence, each containing infinite sub-divisions-seven white notes on your keyboard, with their intermediate tones and harmonics. Someone decided that there should be seven days in a week. I wonder whether they were influenced by the fact that there are seven colours in the rainbow? I can verify that the human body has seven centres of energy, whatever name you wish to give to them. Since the physical body is composed of atoms, all, as Oliver would say, with their negative and positive particles, it would seem common sense to use magnetism to help revitalise those centres that have become rather static. The magnetic lines of force that surround any magnet may be made to fluctuate at different speeds or frequencies, therefore in your modern days the magnets that I would use would be made up of coils of wire wound round an iron core, so that electricity of chosen frequencies could be selected to induce the magnetism. I feel that just as certain radio frequencies achieve different results, especially in their propagation, so magnetic lines of force, made to fluctuate at different frequencies would help stimulate the different nervous systems within the body.

At the same time I agree with my friends that the greatest healing that exists is that which is brought about by the use of one's own mind. Oliver whispers in my ear-" Physician-heal thyself-not by taking an aspirin"!

I realise now that when I attached people to the baquet and used magnets in the shape of bodily organs, it was the belief in both myself and the methods used, that brought about the cures. The biggest enemy of the curative properties of the water of Lourdes is doubt. In my opinion the success of the same water is due to the suggestions as to its effect, by books, religious teachings and those who have succeeded in the art of self suggestion. Maybe those who have achieved levitation have done so by believing that it was possible. Without wishing to offend any religious authority, I 'suggest', that there is a link between self suggestion or faith and the conditions that prevail in the level of consciousness one finds oneself after physical death. From my observation many here still adhere to the same religious faith after death, as they did when living. In some levels, religious services are held and prayers offered to a God that is still personified. Many living suggest to themselves that there is no such thing as an existence after physical death. No wonder then that they stay in a sleep state for an indeterminable time.

It seems a pity that medical science has only recently accepted the reality of the power of suggestion when religions have been using it since the time of the sun god. Ammonia may be placed under the nose of a subject who, under the state of hypnosis is told it is rose water. The eyes do not water, neither is the nasal nervous system upset in any way. If instead, rose water was

45

held under the nose and a suggestion made that it was ammonia, it would be seen that the subject would suffer physically and become emotionally distressed. It is not my purpose to emphasise the curative effects of modern hypnosis but rather to point out the power of self suggestion. The phenomenon of " stigmatisation" , is a result of the brooding on the stigmata of Christ's passion-the power of self suggestion, -or as Oliver might say-the creative ability of the mind. It is well known that the hypnotist can suggest that there is a nonexistent dog on your lap and you will see a dog, very real to you. I mention these things to strengthen the statement made by Oliver, that everything that exists in any level of consciousness does so by the creative mind power of the inhabitants—their power of self suggestion. If these words be true-and they are, then those in our worlds who do not accept communication with your world is possible, will find that it is not. My friends and I work hard with many in our worlds suggesting that communication with those friends on earth is possible. Only when our suggestions are accepted will that communication take place.

My friends here have suggested that not all of you in your earthly world were meant to be mediums. At the same time your bible would state that to one is given one gift and to another, a different gift. All then have gifts. Once again I would like to suggest that doubt is the factor that prohibits the gifts manifesting in some of you.

Post-hypnotic suggestions have a very wide range, not only affecting hearing and sight, but all kinds of vaso-motor responses in cardiac, respiratory, stomachic and other systems of the human organism. Due to doubt, only a few in your living world have learnt how to overcome such conditions as cancer, parkinson's disease and others considered terminable. I want to take this opportunity of encouraging mankind to put aside doubt and to realise that anything is possible by using the power of mind suggestion. How often do you witness an elderly person, free from any illness, decide to die, when they have lost their life partner. Surely if you can decide to die, you can decide to live, and overcome whatever illness befalls you. You are mind and your physical body will respond, through that intermediate etheric vehicle, to all positive commands. It is the negativity in the mind that is responsible for problems both physical and nervous. If I can infringe on the privacy of this instrument's work, it could be related how he placed in his son's mind, in two hours, the mathematical knowledge that normally would have taken a year to learn. How far it is possible to heighten intelligence by the power of suggestion has yet to be discovered.

Let me take the opportunity of answering one of Raymond's many questions-" Is hypnosis used in the "Spirit world". Yes, in the sense that suggestions of truth are made to those whose conception of it is distorted. Not all

46

are 'willing to listen'. In similar fashion to earthly use of hypnosis, we use the power of suggestion to those who are still in sleep state as well as using it as a process of learning with those who are quite conscious. In your earthly world the power of suggestion is used by religions, politics and commercialism for the purpose of deception. How can every motor car be better than every other? How can every cleansing product be the best? The power of suggestion may be used in both your earthly world and ours for either deception or learning greater truths. Surely you realise that there are devious souls in our lower levels of mind, well illustrated sometimes when you use the ouija board. There are low minds here who would try to have you believe misconceptions about our worlds. They do this by suggesting their very limited knowledge through unreliable channels. "Test the Spirit". Mischievousness, lying, and even aggressiveness are not peculiar to only earth entities. I would expect those who are willing to read any of these chapters to analyse the suggestions made, and only accept what appeals to each individual mind. Do not allow yourselves to be 'hypnotised' by any untruths.

We are amazed by the fact that your modern means of communication, radio, television and newspapers seem to suggest that it is right to use guns, to worship sex perversion, materialism and put greater emphasis on the physical than the more permanent spiritual qualities of mind. If I had my way, I would use all of these means to inform mankind of his true reason for manifestation in earthly conditions-to strive for the good rather than worship the evil. Those who put greater emphasis on the physical are creating their own punishment, for here, there is nothing physical-only a mental simulation of it. Oliver's son Raymond soon learnt that etheric whisky and soda did not give the same satisfaction as your earthly alcohol. If he were to continue yearning for such earthly conditions, his only recourse would be to eventually return, to reincarnate until he learnt that spiritual knowledge and advancement gives greater satisfaction than any earthly pleasure. The pleasure derived from the partial penetration involved in sexual activity cannot be compared with the ecstasy of the complete union of two minds; and even this can be excelled when several minds unite as they do in this group of which I am privileged to be a member. When mind transcends to that level called the spiritual spheres and then celestial, then the unification of mind and spirit may then be described as returning to the Godhead. The thoughts that I now express, I do so, not through experience, but through the understanding given to us by that great light who dwells in a higher level than ourselves.

I have learnt now that the passive state, the hypnotic trance may be induced not only by verbal suggestion but telepathically. This is how I am able to place Raymond in a trance like state in which he is more capable of receiving our telepathic transmissions. I do not doubt that I can do this and so

47

it is. You also may induce hypnosis telepathically and use the power of suggestion to those who are not able to be in your presence. It is this power of therapeutic suggestion that takes place in what is termed absent healing. You do not have to rely on your " Spirit Guide"(FRIEND) to do the absent healing for you. You also can do it. I am not belittling help given by your invisible friends but trying to suggest that your mind is just as capable of working at a distance as ours.

I am sure that you have noticed that if you concentrate hard enough on some living person sat or stood in front of you, they will eventually turn their head because they feel the energy transmitted from your mind. They do not need to be even in the same room, county or country, for telepathic transmissions are not limited by distance, speed or time. Oliver's acrostic, " TIN-STAC", There is no such thing as coincidence is true, for how many times have you been thinking of a certain person and that person either knocks at your door or telephones you? Coincidence or telepathy? You can use the power of your mind, not only to achieve physical health but to achieve anything. If only I had understood all of these things when living, my work would have been appreciated rather than deprecated by the medical doctors in Paris. I was not a charlatan-only ignorant of the facts that I now state. Earlier in this chapter I said that through this medium, I feel I am able to rectify some of the ignorance and mistakes of my earthly life. I applaud the choice of book titles made by Oliver and urge those of you who do not want to make similar mistakes in your earthly life-to" read on" -especially those who are, " willing to listen". Thank you for allowing me to add my thoughts to those of my friends. Remember-the words that you read in this book are not our words but only the interpretation of our thoughts; some of your bird or animal friends may not understand human language but can respond to the thoughts transmitted by your mind. I suggest that instead of just accepting these statements you experiment with a friend in a lower kingdom of life. Instead of verbally saying" Come here", or "sit" , to your dog, you think it instead, and with constant practice you will find that telepathy is more universal than any language. Instead of using the words, "I love you"—show it with both your actions and thoughts.Throw out all doubts and negativity. Replace them with positive thoughts of well being, not only for yourself, but also for your friends.Use the power of suggestion, not only in words, but also with your mind, to heal yourself and others.Before standing to one side, I wish to confirm the fact that it was I who transmitted telepathically information as to where my earthly body lay and described it..This enabled an acquaintance of this medium to verify my transmission when he and his companion visited Meersburg.

Thank you for reading on.

FRANZ ANTON MESMER

Harold Smith (Ray Smith's father)

CHAPTER 4

" HELLO-HELLO"

Hello-I'm Raymond's dad. They told me that ad got to think o' some song to start what av got to say. I can't talk as posh as some o' t'others cos they said that when we speak to you, wiv got to talk like we did when we wer there. Ye see, our Raymond went t' college and learnt to speak better than me and May-that's me wife ye know. Anyway-am' ere. Al tell ye what. Al ask our Raymond t' put what' av got to say in good English then y'll know wat' am talking about, but this is what a sound like when 'ave got chance to talk.

Yes, it's true. Our Raymond used to ask his mother and I, whether he would go to heaven when he died. This would be when he was about five years old. I often wondered why he thought about these things for his mother and I never talked about dying. Now I realise more than ever, that he came back into his incarnation so that he could play his part in trying to make some sense of birth, life and death. He would cry if we did not respond to his answers about life after death; and yes it is also true that when he became a choir boy and server in St. Peter's church in Newton-le-Willows, he asked the vicar, a Mr. Broadhurst, the same questions. Even when he did his national service, he would often ask his mother and I to go to some Spiritualist meeting in Warrington, where some medium or other was demonstrating. Sometimes we went, but I must confess that in those days I had more interest in living than dying. In a way, I suppose we let him down.

Although only a plumber, I did have sufficient interest, not only in building, but in electricity, and tried to interest my son in many electrical experiments. I certainly succeeded. We bought him many books to help him understand how things worked. In one particular book, it gave instructions on how to build a gadget that would enable you to hear the buzzing of flies outside the window. This must have been about the time when Raymond was becoming curious about girls, etc. For those who understand a little about electricity, this gadget consisted of the graphite core out of a battery, balanced so that it would rest very delicately on a carbon block, thus making a heath robinson microphone. This was connected in series with an earphone, a battery, and with suitable adjustment to the balance, would pick up the most delicate sounds. Instead of flies, Raymond decided that he would investigate what happened in his mother's and my bedroom, for I found his contraption just outside my bedroom, and was very careful to make sure that he never heard any of the private life of his mother and myself. I did

50

not even mention that I had seen it, and only when he reads this chapter will he know that I knew of his antics. Many times I had to apologise to neighbours to whose daughters my son had written very suggestive letters. In those days his curiosity not only centred on electrical things but naturally on life itself. I'm sure that both he and I realise that this was a necessary chapter of his life-I should have said chapters, for there was not only one. However, as I can now see, this was all because one day he would be able to put the importance of physical life to one side and concentrate more on the Spiritual. Maybe other mediums could tell a similar story.

His interest in music also started when every Sunday, his mother and I would listen to Albert Sandler and his palm court orchestra. I'm sure he hated it at first but eventually came to appreciate it. A friend of mine would come to our house to play the piano, an instrument that I had always wanted to learn to play. In those days, he would go to the cinema with his cousin Leonard to see something like" Old mother Riley". One day his cousin said that he had to go to a music lesson, for he was learning to play the cornet. Raymond went along with him-they were only about nine years old at the time. When Raymomd returned home, he told us of how he listened to his cousin trying to play, and said to his mother and I, " I bet I could play that thing in three weeks better than Leonard after six months. We bought him a cornet-paid five bob for it. It took him longer than three weeks to play better than his cousin, but not that much longer, for his cousin gave up soon after Raymond started to play. By the time he was eleven years old, he had his own dance band. The other members of the band were all adults, so you can tell that he had become quite proficient in his mastery of, by then the trumpet. His knowledge of music was much improved by his joining brass bands. All of the friends that send thoughts to him were involved in music some way or other.

I'm sorry, -it sounds as if I am boasting about my own son, but to be honest, I never appreciated his talent when I was living and this is the only opportunity I have had since I committed suicide in my fifties. I want him to know that I am proud of him and all that he did in his younger life. I'm even more proud of him now that he has devoted his life to serving-not the vicar, but what he calls his invisible friends, Oliver and all the rest of the group here. Now I've got that off my chest, I can tell you the real reason why I have been asked to add my little bit in this book.

I've tried to tell many people how I stuck my head in the gas oven, because I was worried about my broken leg and also because I found my wife, May was playing about. I hoped she would come home in time to find me, but she didn't and here I am. Where am I? ; not in the same place as Oliver and those others but it's quite nice. Whenever they need me to talk at any of their meetings they come for me. I think it would be more correct to say that they come down from where they are and pick me up on the way. It's a bit like dreaming only it's real. All the things that I like are where I am and I suppose I like some of the things that Oliver and his friends don't. Is our Raymond writing this in a way that you can understand? I hope so. At least it's different than the way that the others write. Even though I have asked them to make our Raymond write better than I could, you should still be able to feel that it's me.

When I did away with myself and woke up, my mother and father were there but it was a bit like a dream. It took me a long time to come to. It was like being in a hospital. There were people there looking after us, for there wasn't only me there. When I realised what had happened to me, I was taken to a beautiful place in the country; to a house that I had always dreamed of when I was where you are. There were other people there that seemed to be just as close as my own family and I seemed very happy there. A very beautiful lady would often come and help me to realise that I shouldn't have done what I did. I asked her what I could do about it, but she said that I would one day know what I must do. One day when she was with me, the thought came to me that others might be doing the same sort of thing that I did. I had to try to stop them. As soon as I thought this, it seemed as if other friends naturally joined me, for they had the same sort of feeling. They had either gassed themselves,put a bullet through their brain, taken too many pills or something else daft.

We seem to know when somebody on earth is trying to commit suicide and we try our damnedest to concentrate on them and try to stop them. We don't always succeed, but if we fail and they come here, we try to help them just as others helped us. I've been doing this now for over forty of your years and I enjoy it. I don't think I'll be doing it for ever. You know-there's a lot of things you can't do when you're where you are, either because your wife won't let you or because you don't have enough money to do them things. Well, you can do them here. I have told you how a friend, Dick Grundy, used to come and play the piano for us and how I always wished I could play like him. Well, now I can. Here there are people who will help you to do whatever you want to do, as long as they think it's good for your mind. I've been learning to play the piano and to read music. I was telling June, how I can play the skaters waltz and a lot of that music written by Strauss-you know-like the blue danube. I 'ope our Raymond's spelt it right. Sorry. I hope that our Raymond has spelt it correctly. That doesn't sound like me-does it? Anyway, he's trying his best. You know, when he does this, he's asleep and writing at the same time. How does he do that? It must be very difficult for him, listening to my thoughts and trying to put them in a way that sounds like me.

There's a lot of other things that I never had chance to do when I was in my body, like driving a car. This might sound daft to you, but when you first come here you can do all the things you want to do. It's true that soon you realise you don't need to ride a bike, drive a car-I never went in an aeroplane but I've been in one now-with our Raymond, only he didn't know I was there. You can do whatever your mind wants to do and find somebody else who wants to do the same as you-that's if you want company. I hear a lot of you saying to Oliver and his friends, " Where is your wife". You know, although you might live with a woman and think you're happy, you'll be surprised when you come here. You don't have to stay with anybody. You can be with other people who seem to think more of you than your wife did. It's a different life altogether. If you want to see your mum and dad or your wife you can but it's hard to explain-there are new friends here, who you feel you want to be with more than those that you knew when you were living. Maybe Oliver and his friends can tell you about this better than I can. It seems that learning to live with a family on earth prepares you for a better family here. You know, when you were young like me, you had girl friends, or boy friends if you are a woman. At the time, you thought the world about each one of them until you found somebody better. Then eventually, like me, when you got older you met somebody about the time everybody gets married and so you married somebody, just like I married May. Well, here you keep on meeting different people and it seems to get better and better. You don't have to get married to any of them but just keep on getting more and more friends.

I'm not in the same place as when I first came. I don't need a bike, a car or a plane to get wherever I want to be. I only have to think and it happens. They tell me that that's what happens when you sometimes get out of your body. You go where your mind wants to go. If that sounds strange, it's because you don't always know what your mind really wants to do or where to go. What you lot ought to do you know, is get a lot of questions ready for when Oliver and his friends talk to you, then you'll be more ready for coming here than I was.

I told you that I was a plumber when I was where you are.You'll never believe it. There are still plumbers and carpenters and brickies and everything else here. Some don't even know they've died. It's hard to explain, but honest—if you want to carry on plumbing, you can. You can do anything you want to do. I'm not telling you what some of them get up to— You can imagine. Those who murdered when they were there still try to make others do the same. I mean that just as we try to stop some earthly people not to commit suicide, there are some here who encourage some of you there to murder and do all sorts of terrible things. Not everthing that comes from these places is good. Some maniacs try to make some of you there do what they would like to do. They do it by thinking hard on somebody who likes that sort of thing.

I can see my wife whenever I want. I only have to think and she's there. Sometimes I sort of hear her calling me and I'm with her.I was trying to tell you before—here you carry on meeting people and it keeps getting better and better. I don't only love my wife, my mum and dad, my sisters, Elsie and Ada, but I've learnt to love a lot of other people that I never knew when I was there. Tell our Raymond that Leonard's here now. I met him when he died not long ago. He's not woken up properly yet. That's because when he was there, he didn't think there was anything after death. Anyway 'av got to go— Eh up-here's Oliver and his friends. They'll be telling me to shut up in case I make it sound too good, and you come here before you're ready. I know what they tell you is the truth. Try to make the best of your life whilst you're there then you might find yourself in an even better place than the one I'm in. Even if you get fed up with life like I did, don't do anything daft or you'll find you will want to make up for it, like we do. In a way you have to, before you can go any further. Just before I go, I want to make you laugh and tell you some things that happened when I was living. I've told you that I was a plumber. I used to do all the jobs in the council houses where I lived when I came back from Canada. I went there to try to get a job in the 1930's but I couldn't get one so I came back. Anyway, as I was saying-when I was a plumber, I used to go in houses to do jobs and the ladies there used to offer me a cup of tea—sometimes something else. I used to say, " I never drink tea without biscuits". Do you think I was cheeky? I'm not telling whether I ever got anything else. Sometimes I used to get notes pushed through my letter box saying, " Dear Harold, my leg's come off and I can't wash". That was in the days when they had gas washing boilers. Do any of you remember?. Other notes would ask me if I would go and cut their water off. Depending on who it was, I went and 'cut their water off'. Anyway, I've got to go. Ta, Ra.

Ollie here. I do hope that in the foregoing script transmitted by the father you can see that in telepathic transmissions, not only the thoughts are felt, but also the personality of the communicator. This is why, we felt that by asking Harold to express his thoughts to you, you would be able to feel in the writing that the personality in each case is different. I'm sure that you will extend your sympathy to this medium who has tried to express the Lancashire character of his father in words that are befitting to that character. Whenever, we have the privilege of transmitting our thoughts to you, it is rather like setting the stage, then deciding which actor should first appear.

In large meetings we naturally have to speak in a manner, tone of voice and with the mannerisms that befitted our earthly character. As I have said before, life on earth is rather like the actors of old who used to hold a mask before their face; a mask appropriate to character they tried to portray. None of you in truth show your true personality, soul or mind character when faced with a group of strangers. I don't think, on reflection that I ever displayed my real self even to my own family. Here, there are no masks. The colours displayed in the light of your ethic garments tell all. When the time comes to dispense for ever with those garments, in the mental and spiritual spheres, there will be nothing to hide. Who next then to step onto the stage in these communicative appearances of our assembled ethic actors? Let us see as we draw the curtains on the father's act and set a new scenery for" Act Five". As Harold takes his bow, he wishes me to say that he looks forward to meeting some of you when he is able to have you hear not only his thoughts, but also hear his voice. A standing ovation may even encourage him to appear in one of the following acts.

Dr Charles Richet

CHAPTER 5

" C'EST SI BON"

C'est moi, Je m'appelle Charles Richet. Ah!Il es necessare que j'escribe en englais. Pardonez moi. Yes, my name is Charles Richet and as you can see, I was born in France. If this chapter is to serve any useful purpose, there would seem no point in writing anything that you could read about me, unless it served as a necessary point of reference. In living life, Oliver and I were great friends, not only in our researches into mediumship, but to the extent that we even exchanged sons. This was of course a temporary arrangement, enabling our sons to familiarise themselves with the language of another country. Oliver, Frederick Myers and I shared many interesting experiences and discussions. It is the topics of these discussions that I would like to share with you.

Many of you who are willing to read on must have wondered why it is that at physical birth there seems to be no memory of any previous existence-that all experiences contained within one's mind seem to be relevant to the present incarnation. Those who have read on will be saying that there are exceptions, in the fact that some infants do seem to bring memories with them. Which is the norm? -Those who can remember, or has what is called civilisation robbed man of this ability? It is a logical thought, to wonder how much of you is due to the fact that your physical being is a result of your parents' intercourse. I agree that when you look at a new born baby, whether human or otherwise, it would seem to be devoid of intelligence, experience and wisdom. Is this so? At the same time, we notice that the sense of hunger arises very quickly and even newly born puppies seem to know instinctively the source of mother's milk. It is natural to question where these instincts lie. Are they in the brain or some other organ of the body. Those who study these matters talk of genes and D. N. A. molecules and suggest that certain patterns of life are contained in these microscopic parts of our being. It is also true, that when you eat meat it helps to produce new human cells in your body. If you give a piece of the same meat to your dog, new dog cells are formed. Are these same genes and molecules responsible for this phenomenon one might also ask. Nature displays amazing sights when one has the opportunity to see the newly born animal rise to it's feet within seconds of birth. Man tends to stick a label of 'self preservation instinct' on this phenomenon without really understanding it's origin.

Oliver has talked about the elemental, vital, ethic, astral, mental, spiritual and celestial levels. Common sense would tell us that the law and order within the atom must have come from somewhere. Oliver and other

57

scientists taught their students that every atom consisted of protons and electrons-electrical charges. No scientist really knows exactly what a proton is. They feel that they have sufficient evidence to state that every proton is positive, but for all they know that proton may also be the seat of consciousness. In the same way, religions suggest that God is love, yet they fail to give a true definition of love. or of God.

The terms conscious, sub-conscious, super-conscious, unconscious and racial consciousness have been used by both men of religion and science yet I feel that these terms have never been adequately defined. We have much to learn. In the same way, your modern scientists are gradually becoming aware that each atom not only consists of the elements of matter, but also contain strange behaving particles, that for the moment simply mystify them, for they seem to be infinite in their number. Many of the particles that they observe, seem to be able to pass through what they have defined as matter, and also seem to conform to laws outside the realms of ordinary physics. Because of this they have extended the branches of physics to now include such terms as quantum mechanics, finding that when two of their particles collide, two constituents of light called photons appear and what is more, seem to behave in identical manner. The number of theories, hypotheses and explanations exceed the number of prevailing religions and in truth science is just as lost as religion in its effort to explain these things. In his thoughts, Oliver and other friends here often refer to infinite levels of consciousness-and yet-can any of us claim to truly understand the word infinite. Words may sound" grande" , but the idea of education is surely to give an understanding of the works of both nature and science, -of God. Maybe I should not use the term God, for not one person that I know has any definite understanding of that term.

Should the different levels of consciousness only be applied to man, or can we include other manifestations of life-even the microbe? The white corpuscles of the body seem to work quite independently, dashing off to war against any foreign invaders. Who or what trained them to do this? Without delving too much into man's biological make up, it can be seen that man himself consists of many such systems all behaving independently, except when the occasion arises when joint co-operation is needed. What part does consciousness play in the motor systems of the body? Do you need a soul, spirit or whatever to urge the white corpuscles to do their work? Maybe they are subject to greater systems within the body and they in turn respond to the existing layers of mind, the highest called spirit. Oliver draws a parallel to the individual members of an orchestra, who form part of one section. All the sections play together under the skillful hand of the conductor. It must be admitted that some conductors are better than others-some minds are better

58

and more capable of controlling sub-levels and thence the physical. I have been asked by the group here to express my thoughts in simplicity, therefore I crave the indulgence of readers who may have an extensive knowledge of biology.

The close friend of this medium, Franz upset the medical authorities when in about 1750 he suggested that 'animal magnetism' could be passed through the fingers of one to another in a system of therapeutic healing. Unfortunately he stepped outside the boundaries of credulity when he connected his patients to iron rods produding out of tubs of metal. At the same time I feel that credit should be given to him for at least suggesting there were forces outside the laws of physics that could be used in such processes as healing. Another member of our group whose name is Armand furthered Franz's work and was probably the forerunner of your today's hypnosis in which certain levels of consciousness are either heightened or subdued. Myers, a great friend of both Oliver and myself did extensive research into telepathy, another phenomenon outside physical science; from these remarks you will see that the group that gather around this medium, do so because they recognise his intense interest in these levels of consciousness. He is a bird of the same feather.

I realise that I have digressed somewhat, but wanted to emphasise and explain why we find Raymond a suitable person for our continued study of these matters.

I feel that readers may be prepared to agree that the various terms applied to consciousness are not all relevant to the atom. Since law and order are the first signs of intelligence, we could then say that each atom displays a birth of mind in it's elemental stage of development. Elemental mind must have some vehicle-a mineral in which it can manifest for us to become aware of it. In this level, genes and D. N. A. are not necessary. I refer to the mineral kingdom. Next to appear on the stage of creation, is life, that not only requires elemental mind but also the vital principle which houses the genes and other molecules that contain the pattern of the type of life, whether it be a fish, bird, insect or human. The many manifestations of life illustrate the fact that the architect is still at his drawing board designing. Some seem to have been put in the waste basket as with the dinosaurs and other extinct creatures. The elementary and vital forms of mind then are only necessary when life first emerges from the mineral kingdom.. The forces within the elementary and vital can be passed from parent to child, from bitch to puppy, from cat to kitten-ad infinitum. Next in Oliver's list came the etheric. Kirlian photography suggests that even the mineral world has an etheric counterpart; so has the vegetable and plant world, for the ether is the link between the mind world and the physical. It is the medium through which the designer sends his plans to the builder. These plans manifest physically in those atoms, genes and molecules and the cells of the body. In the vital world, law and order has added to itself other complex molecules which help it reproduce and even improve itself as well as preserve it's own species. The instinct of self preservation is only one of many instincts in the vital level of mind. I'm sure that Oliver, in his first book made reference to the creeping vine and the Venus fly catching plant, both of which seem to have a sense of direction, even though they lack a brain. These senses or instincts can be seen to be passed to their offspring, often in a seed, an egg or in your case, a foetus. In other words, the new born baby benefits from the elementary and vital evolution of mind. Even these lower aspects of mind evolve. It is not those parts of mind- that join the foetus in mother's womb.

Neither a stone nor a blade of grass is conscious of it's own existence in the same way as we are. As we move gradually to the next level of physical manifestation-the animal world-your world, it can be seen that other levels of mind, under the watchful eye of the architect, adds to those elementary and vital levels. Your dog, cat or other such pet, displays not only the emotional level of mind, but even seems to have another layer called imagination. Dogs dream. In some animals, especially those high up in the kingdom, a sense of reasoning can be observed as well as the first signs of love. The architect's design of creation is gradually taking shape, as mind adds to itself layer after layer. Only when love has reached a sufficient strength, can mind become conscious of it's own being. Is the worm, to which Oliver referred in his book, conscious of it's own being or here, does consciousness mean that it is able to move, eat and reproduce. Here, I repeat that consciousness needs greater clarification, as does sub-consciousness, etc. , etc. It is true that parents may pass on to their children or grandchildren those patterns that are physically stored in the elementary and vital part of their makeup, but what about those higher levels of mind? Where is seated the imagination, a sense of beauty, emotion and feelings of love. ? Which part of the mind receives premonitions and is able sometimes to exteriorise itself from the body? -from the elementary and vital? Which part of the mind is responsible for telepathy and even memory? If the dead do really exist in some other dimension, as suggested by various forms of mediumship, then it would appear that the qualities of emotion, beauty, imagination, intelligence, memory, wisdom and love persist and are not in any way, part of our physical being, but of something else-those layers of mind that are higher than the elemental and vital. These are the levels of mind that join the seed, the egg and the foetus. In the latter case, those levels of mind have developed sufficiently to be individualised. I'm sure Oliver would say that the cohesion between these higher levels had reached sufficient strength to give a viscosity sufficient to enable them to remain separate globules of mind.

Many children resemble their relatives physically but not necessarily in personality. If some do, it could be that the child has adopted certain mannerisms that appealed to it, and therefore not passed on genetically. Even a parrot, monkey, horse and other creatures can imitate.

Certain levels of mind then do not need any physical vehicle in which to reside, but are forms of energy in a much higher state of vibration than that which lives in the elementary and vital. When in earthly conditions I and my friends here were conscious of our being. We still are. In our consciousness we could delve deeper than the sensations given by the five senses and remember previous experiences. We had memory, imagination, intelligence, a sense of humour, emotion, reason and love. We still have the same facets of mind but would find it very hard to express them through a new vehicle (reincarnation); we would have to wait until that vehicle developed. In modern terms, we are the programme, but have to wait for the computer to grow before we can display the full content of our programme. What is more, that programme becomes more extensive or complicated with every experience-with every incarnation. Sometimes it might be necessary for us to experience having a computer of limited capability so that our minds can experience the frustration of that limitation.

A stone then has a body, but only contains the elementary level of mind. The plant and vegetable kingdom exhibits elementary, vital and the infancy of higher levels. Maybe that Venus fly catching plant compared with a blade of grass, illustrates the fact that even in this kingdom there are infinite levels. Without reference to any particular animal, it can be seen that this kingdom also gives mind an opportunity to strive for individuality, that state displayed in the highest of the animal world-human.

This is only the beginning of an experience. Earthly incarnations are opportunities to grow wings so that we may fly in that butterfly world-the spirit world, where we may have experiences that the limitations of earthly existence prevent.

Just as the mineral kingdom, plant , vegetable and animal kingdoms provide mind with an opportunity to develop to an individualised state, so the seven spheres of our world give that individualised mind opportunities to strengthen itself so that it may leave the butterfly world and find even greater freedom. Where? God's creation is infinite and therefore opportunities for strengthening individuality are also infinite.

Whether physiologist, scientist, marquis, nun, monk, plumber or mesmerist, we in this group realise that in earthly life our attention was mainly focused on physical and material matters. Earthly qualifications mean nothing here, for they only apply to our last incarnation. The father of this medium is just as spiritual as any of us, for spirituality is a gathering of the harvest of ones total evolution of mind. Do not therefore pay greater respect to any one of us more than another for we are all essential atoms of the same molecule of mind. In manifesting through this channel we, of necessity take on the mask of personality that earthly friends expect. Raymond's father is more qualified to express his thoughts on suicide than any other member of the group. Each one of us help to set up the stage, then take part in the presentation of the play, "birth, life and death". We understand that you, naturally expect us to play the part that we rehearsed in our last incarnation. If we were to act the part we played in a previous incarnation it would serve no useful purpose.

When we are privileged to express our thoughts through this medium, some would ask us about our previous lives. Although a refusal may seem devious, except the fact that we may not be proud of the things we did or did not do in our last but one entry upon that earthly stage of life. It is our pleasure to share the knowledge and experiences that we feel would be of benefit to your time spent in the prison of earthly conditions. It would serve no useful purpose for you to know whether I manifested as a rose or daffodil in the evolution of my mind. In the same way, whether I was a professor or murderer in my last entry in the play of life is a personal fact which enables me to more understand what I am now. In saying this, I encourage you to become aware of the experiences or lives you have had, for this will help in the expression, " Man, know thyself". Just as there may be certain experiences in your living life, that you for the moment wish to keep to yourself, we too are not that much different.

It has already been stated that we are all interested in what is called hypnosis-the taking away of inhibitions and the revealing of the true colours of the mind. It is true that not all good subjects are willing to reveal their previous lives in that process called regression. Some do not even want to remember the earlier part of their present incarnation for it holds too many bad memories. Only certain special people are willing to reveal the secrets of their spiritual education.

We have a difficulty. The more this medium friend of ours is able to express our thoughts, the more it appears as if we were actually speaking. Oliver has adequately explained that all communication is telepathic. Although we are able to have this medium speak our thoughts, we find it very difficult to have him speak actual words. Do not be surprised then if he found difficulty in giving the name of my wife or the names of my sons. Thoughts are relatively easy to transmit but actual words are not. We do not jump into his body and pull the strings. A better comparison would be telekinesis-the movement of objects by mind energy. This may only be demonstrated by very few incarnate and discarnate minds.

The mineral kingdom is more complex than when it first manifested on your earth. It took a long time for gem stones to evolve. As stated by Oliver, the plant and vegetable world is more advanced than when it first appeared. It is not surprising then, to find that in the animal kingdom, including human form, evolved mind has demanded more complex vehicles. All levels of mind are constantly progressing and what is more; there is an infinite supply of the essence of mind. The mind of mankind, will eventually not need to use a physical body, but will put it to one side, just like the butterfly discards the cocoon. No doubt the mind of the butterfly will have the opportunity to have experiences in the numerous species in the bird kingdom before moving ever onwards through other kingdoms where mind can gain individuality. What lies ahead for us in the next sphere of consciousness is as far away from our understanding as the butterfly world is from the understanding of the caterpillar. Those in the seventh sphere have little conception as to the experiences available for mind in other parts of God's infinite creation.

Try to understand the place in which you now dwell and have your being before trying too much to understand our worlds. Be content to know of their reality. The nursery school student knows of the existence of the infant school but does not understand everything in it. We have passed from the nursery school of earth into the infant school of the mind and are trying hard to understand it. Those higher levels of the mind world, the spirit and celestial regions are beyond our understanding. We are told a little about them, just as we try to tell you about our level, but our minds are not yet ready to appreciate their full beauty. A willingness to learn is the only pathway of progression, therefore take what opportunities you have whilst on earth then you might not fail your self-examination and have to repeat another session in earth's nursery school. Ignorance is not bliss-' tis wise to be wise. Free yourself from the fantasies and superstitions of those who pretend to know the truth. Find it for yourself. Remember the fact that every cell of your body can live without you.In living life I conducted experiments which proved this statement to be a fact. At the moment they serve the purpose of contributing towards the vehicle that you drive.Drive well through all the avenues of life. Respect the lower minds in each cell of your body and take the opportunity to observe the beauty of earth's garden. Only when you do this will you be able to realise that the beauty of the mind and spirit worlds is superior.

Au-revoir.
CHARLES

CHAPTER 6

"ME AND MY SHADOW".

My mind once more like a wireless transmitter beams thoughts through the ether to the receiver hoping that the frequencies are in the same wave band for those thoughts to be transcribed.

I am pleased that my friend Charles referred to the difficulty in having those thoughts expressed or written in exact words. Although I have previously referred to the difficulties in communication, I must once again emphasise that how my thoughts are transcribed, often depends on the physical, mental and spiritual state of this medium at the time of transmission. Should there be any mistakes, forgive him for he, like you, is subject to the trials of physical incarnation. His computer sometimes has a virus—meaning that his physical being is not in a fit state to interpret the thoughts that we transmit. The higher parts of mind to which Charles referred, need the elemental and vital to be in good condition so that thought may express itself in a manner that all can understand. If they are not, then often people are classed as either physically or mentally handicapped.

The group, of which I am just part, are aware of the thoughts of Raymond. Not all are correct, yet his observations provide us with valuable information. Telepathy is a two way process.Messages are not only received from our worlds to yours, but even more so from your world to ours. Because of this we are aware that a group of friends are eager to know what lies at the end of spiritual progress, through the seven spheres with their infinite sub-divisions. I therefore take the liberty to express one or two thoughts with regards to this quest. Where are we all going? May I first remind you of transmissions already sent with regards to from where we all came.

In the previous book, and even in this one, reference has often been made to the progress of mind from its elementary vibrations in the mineral kingdom, to those higher states displayed in the animal kingdom-your kingdom. The mineral kingdom with its many atomic and molecular compositions demonstrates the first stirring of the ether and the cohesive, electrical, magnetic and gravitational forces that are necessary for this kingdom to exist in the form of matter. Before this took place ether could be said to be in a state of statisticity; existing but not vibrating, therefore in a sense you have always existed. There are much higher vibrations in the ether, such as those used to form etheric coverings in all forms of life, thus the etheric world covers a vast range of frequencies. When we have referred to the elemental, vital, astral, etheric, mental, spiritual and celestial parts of

64

you, your etheric naturally consists of vibrations in the higher section of that etheric world.

The vital world is just another section of these etheric frequencies, the section where those elementary forces have added to themselves that which we call life. The complex organisms ranging from the virus to the human, demonstrate the fact that this vital world is also vast in its range of frequencies. As my friend Charles stated, this vital world contains the lower parts of what is termed mind; -the parts of mind necessary for the preservation of species, propagation of species and other parts of mind that focus entirely on the physical manifestation of life. The vital within the amoeba is lower than that within the plant and vegetable world where fertilisation is necessary. Not even death was necessary in those days when only such creatures as the amoeba and virus existed on earth. By using the intellectual level of mind, it can be seen that what is termed death was part of a great plan, which necessitated the gradual formation of physical senses, in the increasing manifestations of life. Only by introducing death into the scheme of things could there be room for the development of the vehicles of life.as they are today. Even the fish, bird, and insect worlds show the gradual evolvement of the vital, for now male and female genders appear. The vital world is slowly preparing to add to itself aspects of mind that do not have to dwell in the physical. Somewhere in this chain of life, especially in the animal kingdom, comes the birth of those higher qualities of mind called reasoning, intellect, emotion, character, personality and the greatest of all-love. It is of course these higher vibrations of mind that are independent of the physical and survive what is called death. They make use of physical bodies to develop mind to a stage when it could then be called, " Spirit". Surely, when reference is made to 'the sprit of a person', it would refer to the qualities just mentioned. Just like the proverbial spider 'Try, try again', it can be seen that the animal kingdom is struggling to develop mind to a sufficient strength, enabling it to stay individualised. Only then should the term 'spirit', be used. In other words, the lower kingdoms of life have mind to different degrees of development, but do not have 'spirit', as I have defined it. In my definition, mind is only temporary individual but 'spirit' is permanent.

The only difference between you and me, is the fact that we have left behind the elementary and vital- the shell that encapsulates higher vibrations of mind or spirit and provides it with an opportunity for learning. As the great light would say-we have left the caterpillar world where we had to crawl. Now we exist in a greater freedom-the butterfly world. If the butterfly could reason and think in a manner similar to mankind, I'm sure it would say, " What next" ? -just as you may ask; just as we may ask. I and my friends have tried to communicate some of the conditions that prevail in our level. We have explained that here in our level of mind, there is no need for language. There are no limitations of speed, distance or time. The world of matter presents no barrier to us; in fact we have to lower our mental vibrations to even become re-aware of it. Similarly, those in higher regions of mind, have to lower their mental frequency to become re-aware of ours.

Because we have passed through the portals of death, we are now sure that we are on an infinite journey. To where? Since there is no end to infinity, it is not possible for anyone to define an end. Those who dwell in higher levels than ourselves, tell us that our primitive ideas of love will for ever grow greater as we pass through and beyond the seven spheres of consciousness. I therefore suggest to this medium and his friends that since there is no end, it would be futile looking for it. Be content that you will for ever be able to say, " I am" , and that every time it is said, the 'am' will be wiser, therefore more spiritual. Is it not true to say that the mind of mankind today is greater than the mind of primitive man? A study of the animal world reveals the fact that levels of mind in elementary and vital levels have progressed. Man's immune system has become more efficient. Instincts such as self preservation have also reached a higher level. Most species can offer to their offspring a far better vehicle than was offered millions of years ago. Some progress has been made. Why should the progression of mind and spirit have an end? Since God's creation is infinite, the opportunities for learning are also infinite. You can rest in any stage of the journey, but will find that even resting can become weary. Those who seek an end are really questioning God's purpose of creation. Why did God create matter? Why did life enter it? I suggest that whatever God may be, God is also expanding infinitely and that we are just part of that infinite expansion.

Many in your world and ours, are inspired to postulate what experiences lie on this infinite journey. Inspiration is not only from our worlds to yours. We too are sometimes inspired, and may share that inspiration with you. I understand that not only musicians, artists, writers, scientists and poets receive inspiration, but others who are given a glimpse of what lies on that infinite journey. Some express their inspiration as a journey in space, where they meet intelligences who no longer need to manifest in the physical. They seem to have far greater powers than exist in either our worlds or yours. Some of your space films illustrate the inspiration received by the writers. This is just their interpretation of thoughts given to them with regards to future experiences. We find it very difficult to accurately describe to you our world. Those who dwell in more progressed levels of mind find it equally difficult to describe their world to us. How then can we try to postulate an end that does not even exist?

To this medium and his friends, I suggest that your eyes may be focused a little too much on the limited material world of matter and self. This is not judgement or criticism. Turn your vision to the infinite journey of the spirit on which their are far greater opportunities and purposes than those presented to the physical body. Only a few escape from the boundary of the physical body and have a glimpse of one of our worlds. When they return they often say that they can find no words to describe the visions and feelings that they had. Some even say that they became aware of the mysteries and secrets of God's creation whilst outside their bodies, but could not bring back memory of their illumination. I sympathise with you all, for I remember having similar thoughts when serving my earthly sentence. It seems that the creator, in his wisdom, her wisdom or it's wisdom knew that it was necessary to put us all in a state of enquiry and wondering. This applies to both yourselves and ourselves, no matter in which level of mind we dwell-here or there.

As we become more aware of God's purpose of creation, we move further away from possibilities of sharing our thoughts with you. I'm sure that communication between one level and another was meant to be at least very difficult, if not impossible. Good communication is the exception rather than the rule. Whilst you try to understand objects in your sky and patterns in your fields, we in our worlds are given many mysteries to solve. As mind evolves, the complexity of these mysteries becomes greater; infinitely greater. " Not for you to reason why- just for you to do and die, then like us continue to wonder why. "

The thoughts that we have just expressed may not give much comfort to Raymond and his friends. We do not have all the answers. Let it be a comfort to us all- the fact that we are all on an adventure, that we will always be, that we will understand more as we continue on that infinite journey. Surely this is better than the end some religions suggest-sitting on a gold pavement, playing a harp. That, to me would be hell instead of heaven. We in this group have excepted infinity even though we do not understand it. My son Raymond joins us once again, trying to paraphrase my thoughts in the form of another poem

> Ask us not wherefore or why,
> We only know that we did not die.
> All the things that we did in life,
> Most of them full of trouble and strife,
> Making us many times shed a tear,
> And wonder why God brought us here.
> Where did we come from? Where is it we go?
> Who can tell us what we want to know?

Is life's purpose just to work?
For many from it seem to shirk.
Does all that we've Learned go to waste?
What was the point of trying to be chaste?
Some of those answers you will only find,
Here in our world, the world of the mind.
You may think that your world is real,
When in truth you haven't even begun to feel,
The love that God gives to both you and me,
He doesn't even charge, it's all given free.
Look away from the earth then you'll see
That you go on and on for eternity.

I realise that philosophy, whether expressed in poetry or prose is sweet to the ear but the group assemble here, not to whisper sweet nothings, not to spoil you with pleasantries, but to help and encourage you to enter your level of consciousness with a 'spirit' of continued enquiry and excitement-to enjoy the adventure of both life and afterlife.

Let us try to use a little of what we know in science to support the idea of continued existence after physical death, not only for mankind but for all kingdoms including the mineral. Energy is perpetual, continuing without loss even though sometimes changing its form. The sun constantly loses matter by radiating energy into space. Earth makes use of this radiative energy in order to increase its matter. Your modern scientists have discarded many theories, including the conservation of matter, for now they realise that many stars are disintegrating into radiation. Although matter cannot remain in any permanent state, it is now understood that there is a constant interchange between matter and energy. I suggest that even the law conservation of energy is now suspect. In simplicity, you may feel that at the moment you are your body. After physical death you will find that the real you existed as an energy which simply made use of the physical body. The vibrational state of that energy will determine whether you now call yourself astral, etheric, mind, spirit or celestial being, for these are all states of energy. We cannot tell you what we will call ourselves after the celestial state of being. I find it hard to find a word to describe what lies beyond these states of energy. Energy is certainly supreme to matter. What then is supreme to energy-ad infinitum.

You then are not your body, but rather the space that lies within every atom of your body and even around it. The degeneration of your body simply releases that space from being associated with matter-with your body. Whether you be called mind, spirit, angel or whatever, depends on the quality or frequential vibration of your space energy. We in our group feel that we are mind, struggling to become spirit. In the English language 'spirit' and ' spiritual', are surely noun and adjective belonging to the same origin. In a play with words, it could be said that to become a 'spirit', one should be 'spiritual'. We are trying.

In religions, reference is often made to body mind and spirit, as if there were only the three states of being, but body can refer to something inanimate or animate. The term body then can be sub-divided into elemental and vital. In similar manner the term mind covers existence in astral, etheric and mental levels. The term spirit then encompasses the vibrations in both spiritual and celestial levels. Two plus three plus two equals seven. Not that there is such a thing as coincidence, yet the number seven seems to apply to so many things in both your world and ours. Maybe in book three, we will all have progressed to a level of mind enabling us to suggest a reason for this. I do hope that in this play with words you see that we still retain a sense of humour, which I hope to retain and improve on each step of this infinite adventure.

Whenever we have the privilege of transmitting thoughts to groups of people through our friend Raymond, we always like to try to answer the questions asked by those present. In reading this book, you are reading the thoughts that I and my friends wish to express. We may not even write about those matters that interest each reader, therefore we feel that some chapters in this book should be devoted to some of the answers we have given in the past, present and, I pray future. When you read the answers, remember the fact that the member most befitted to answer will do so. Let us start now.

OLIVER

CHAPTER 7

ANSWER ME?

QUESTION. 1. If God is a God of love, why does he allow all the acts of aggression, war, jealousy and other atrocities to go on?

ANSWER. Your question implies the fact that you still personify God. In other words you feel that God is a person. Is this true?

Yes?

ANSWER CONTINUED. In that case, sir, you and I disagree about the personification of God. All are entitled to their feelings with regards to God. There are indeed many in our worlds who still feel that God is a person and hold religious services worshipping 'him'. If you have read any of the thoughts that we have expressed on this matter you would know that we would rather define God as infinite intelligence. Thoughts from any level in our worlds have to rely on telepathy as a means of communication. It is true that many here try to impinge their thoughts of peace, harmony and love on those who dwell in more animalistic levels of mind, whether in our worlds or yours. If you were limited to this means of communicating with one another, do you feel that your friends would hear your thoughts? Usually, those in lower levels of mind, concentrate on the more material and physical aspects of life, involving greed, jealousy and selfishness. They are deaf, not only to your thoughts but also to ours-also to God. These mental diseases can be seen even in religions that still fight and try to dominate one another, therefore closing the doors of sensitivity and spiritual values. As we have said, so many times, earthly life is a school of learning in which there is an opportunity to witness the yin and the yang-the positive and the negative. Unless you had the opportunity of seeing the actions of those who dwell in those lower levels of mind, you would never be able to appreciate the peace, wisdom and spirituality of those who dwell in higher levels. Take comfort in the fact that when you leave your physical world, you will dwell in a level where all are of similar mind to yourself. Make sure then that your mind level is one that desires peace, tranquillity, harmony, knowledge wisdom and love; a level in which religious superstition has been replaced by knowledge, truth, understanding and love. If it is your continued desire to think of God as a person, then you will join others who think the same. Whatever God may be, God bless you for allowing us to share our thoughts with you. (The group).

QUESTION. 2. When does the spirit join the body after conception and what happens in the case of a miscarriage or an abortion?

ANSWER. The spirit joins the body at the moment of conception—at the same time as the sperm succeeds in penetrating the egg, but does not necessarily stay close to the foetus. Just as you often leave your body during sleep, always joined by the etheric umbilical chord, the spirit in that foetus leaves the newly forming body. As the term of pregnancy continues the spirit stays for longer periods until the time of quickening, when it would stay close to the body for about the same time as you stay close to yours. The link formed at conception is a permanent one. If the mother aborts then it is similar to you taking the life of another. The spirit is forced to return to that level of mind from whence it came. Sometimes the spirit may grow faint hearted and shrink from the trials of another incarnation. You may, in this case say the child was stillborn. The spirit and mind of a person can decide to die, or should I say leave, from the time it is born to even old age. Is it not true that in the case of two very close and elderly people, when one dies, the other seems to follow very soon after, even though there is no apparent illness. The case of miscarriage could be compared with natural death, when the body is not sufficiently strong to sustain life. The spirit needs mind and life in order to both express itself as well as gather the harvest of incarnate experiences. In the case of miscarriage, the link between parents and child is never lost. The same soul often tries to manifest to the same parents, providing there is another pregnancy. (Teacher and Charles)

QUESTION. 3. In your talking, you said that instead of being a person, God is supreme or infinite intelligence. What proof is there of this infinite intelligence?

ANSWER. It would be appropriate to answer this question with the words of a song-? Nothing comes from nothing?. The works of man in both art and science could be said to be truly marvellous. Mankind in its evolution has been responsible for many wonders, but had to have the material and tools of his trade-the minerals provided by the earth. Man is not responsible for the works of creation, the solar systems, galaxies and the infinity of space. To whom or what then can we attribute creation? It would be wrong to use one unknown in an effort to try to define another unknown. For the moment, both you and I have to accept the premise, that something must have been responsible for all the wonders in creation that are not the works of man. In our search for a suitable description of the cause of everything, we can only find the terms infinite intelligence or in one word-God. There must have been a cause for all that is not the works of man and God was that cause. (Oliver)

QUESTION. 4. My cat was as close to me as any human being, and I was very upset when it died. Will I be able to see Cleo again and will she be just the same as when she died?

ANSWER. Your particular animal friend received great love during its life. The love that you gave it strengthened the levels of mind that are responsible for individuality, therefore you will see her again. Animals and other forms of life exist in your earthly world even though they are not of the same level of mind as yourself. Our worlds would be rather dull if there were no trees, flowers, birds, fish, animals and many other features of earthly conditions. These only exist because of the love transmitted by mind. We have stated that all here exists by the creative ability of mind. Those in lower levels, who may have no appreciation of flowers will find no flowers. The mind of your cat has not evolved to the same level as your own, therefore one day your love will grow strong enough to allow the mind of your cat to progress. It may only do this by returning to its deserved level. You will realise that your love gave it only temporary ability to exist in your level of mind. To love only one cat is a limitation of love. To love only one fellow human is a similar limitation. As our minds progress to a more spiritual level, we will learn to love and appreciate everything in creation equally, irrespective of its level of mind. Mankind often uses the expression, ? he, she or it's mine?. This is possessiveness, not love. It is true love that never dies. The love that you gave your cat should have been given to help it evolve-not so that you could possess it for ever. (Teacher, Charles and Armand).

QUESTION. 5. Can you tell us the truth about flying saucers and patterns in the corn fields?

ANSWER. We can tell you the truth as we have been told it, for higher intelligences than ourselves are responsible for these phenomena. Ever since life in this part of creation gained individuality, those who have left earthly confinement have tried to influence the minds of those left behind. In ages past, they have managed to vibrate the ether so as to present a vision of themselves. When physical energy has been in abundance, some have used it to create physical phenomena. All these things have been done in an effort to convince mankind of continued existence, yet for all but a few, mankind seems to prefer to attribute mysteries to some physical cause. Higher levels of mind are aware of man's desire to conquer space, and therefore take the opportunity of presenting phenomenon in space-in your skies. Patterns have appeared in deserts, ice and fields in ages past, but now those levels of mind are trying to stimulate man's mind to link the two together and ask, " Can those objects in the sky create the patterns that we see. Who is doing this". I suggest to you that if lower intelligences can mischievously move objects in your homes, then higher intelligences can cause the mind of mankind to realise that not everything has an earthly explanation. This explanation only suffices in the times when many see the same vision at the same time. There are those who by their intense desire can create a mental vision for themselves. That is why visions in the sky do not give sufficient evidence of higher intelligent intervention. Patterns in deserts, ice and fields can not for the moment be attributed to incarnate minds.

QUESTION. 6. Before my mother died she promised to return and give me proof of her continued survival. Why has she not done this?

ANSWER I can only repeat what has already been written by Oliver. Your mother's means of communication is limited to telepathy. Although in dream state you seem to manage to communicate without language-mind to mind, incarnate consciousness, because of the five physical senses, seems to take away mental communication. Mankind suggests to himself, because of his technological advances that he is more civilised now than in ages past, yet your ancestors in that distant past did not need your modern means of communication. In those days long ago, telepathy was part of everyday life. Just as you have special religious festivities to acknowledge the teachings of Buddha, Jesus, Mohammed, Confucius and others, tribes of the past accepted communication with our worlds as natural. On special days such as the anniversary of a friends passing into our worlds, a feast was shared to celebrate the rebirth of that friend. It was a joyous occasion-not a sad one. Your mother tries, but finds the materialism and physical emphasis of earthly conditions an impenetrable barrier. One day you may be fortunate to be in the company of one who can feel the thoughts of your mother. Pray then that those thoughts are interpreted in such a manner that you are able to conclude the fact that your mother was the origin of their transmission. You can help by putting the barriers of doubt to one side and opening the door of your mind, so as to let the thoughts of your friend flow freely through both your mind and the mind of the medium.

(A spiritual brother)

QUESTION. 7. We are told that as we travel through your worlds, we discard many bodies and eventually become light. How can we still be individuals if we are all light?

ANSWER. First allow me to remind you that in earthly life there are many features that allow you to recognise one another; the differences of bodily features, faces, fingerprints, lines on the hands, mannerisms and many others. Generally speaking, most who pass into our worlds bring with them an etheric duplicate of that earthly body and therefore recognition of one another presents no problem, although the mind can use that level called memory and mould the etheric body into any age and state of health that is required for recognition. Moving onwards to that time of evolvement

73

when many mind bodies have been shed and the individual becomes just light, let me remind you that the light in all our spheres has a different frequency. The luminosity of the light in those different spheres is infinite in its intensity. In the higher spheres, individuality is retained and displayed by the frequency and brightness of each persons light. Let your light shine before all so that even in earthly life others may recognise you, not by your body, but rather by the light of your mind and spirit. Individuality will always be retained, but gradually its importance fades. We are quite happy to be just a part of the consciousness in which we dwell, no individual trying to outrank another, but all trying to better themselves so that they can be of greater service to others. One could say-of greater service to God. Every atom in a piece of metal is quite happy to be part of the whole. Each cell of your body contributes towards your whole, without any single cell wanting to be better than another. As we all progress we become photons of spiritual light,still individuals,but happy to be part of creation without any thought of trying to outshine another.The group)

QUESTION. 8. You have told us that the colours in your worlds are brighter than those on earth. Can you explain how this can be?

ANSWER. The colours in your world are produced by the fact that everything receives light from your physical sun and some things are more capable of reflecting one of the seven colours than any of the others. A similar principle is involved in all our worlds, but remember the fact that we do not rely on a physical sun for light. As one moves through the spheres, the spiritual origin of the light in each grows brighter, and thus you have heard that our colours are more radiant than those on earth. This is only true in levels where the general level of mind is greater than the average incarnate level. There are of course those who dwell in very low levels of mind, where the spiritual light is so dim that colour cannot even be seen. Whenever you listen to the communications from our worlds, it is important for you to know the level of mind in which your spiritual friend dwells. Just as you have been told that colour here is brighter, I am sure you have heard that time does not exist in the 'Spirit world'. Time does exist for those who dwell in levels very close to earth-earthbound. As you progress, colours grow brighter, time, distance and speed fade into insignificance. Past, present and future are all equally accessible. Other colours such as silver and gold appear in spiritual spectrums of light, and even they have infinite intensities of radiance. (Oliver/Phillipe)

QUESTON. 9. Will you tell us more about what happens to those who commit suicide?

ANSWER. Yes, for we have one amongst us who can speak from experience. (Group)

74

Hello, my name is 'arold, Raymond's dad. First let me explain that when we can come an' speak or write, we try to come in a way that you'll know us. I don't have to write o' speak with a Lancashire accent any more. I don't need to speak. I just think and our Raymond writes. It's same for everybody here. Oliver isn't as posh or as clever as he sounds. He just thinks in a different way than I do. Anyway, you already know that I did away with myself-that sounds daft, doesn't it cos 'am 'ere. I'm sure I've already talked about this when they asked me to write some at earlier on. I didn't come into any dark place. I came into't same place as them who didn't do what I did. Apart from me mum and dad meeting me, there was 'ell of a crowd and amongst 'em were many friends who'ad died before me. There were some there who seemed to stand out more than t'others. They seemed to shine, and you got the feeling that you wanted to talk to 'em. You know, when yer living there's always some people you find you want to be with more than others. Anyway, me mum and dad said that 'ad better 'av a rest first and they'd be there when a woke up. I felt tired anyway and they took me to a beautiful place. Yer know, 'ave always liked to be in t' country an that's were they took me. It looked like Wales. Anyway when I woke up, me mum and dad were there as well as them others that stood out. We talked, I don't know how long- about what 'ad done an' why I did it. They seemed to understand and didn't even blame me-well, not so much. I can't tell yer 'ow long we stayed there but bye'd time we finished a knew a shouldn't 'av done it. Am I writing too much-anyway tell me if I am. I seemed to know a lot of things after they'd finished talking-like stealing. Yer know them who steal cos the've nothin' to eat don't feel as bad as them who steal who don't need it. Well, it's a bit like that. For, me, I didn't seem to feel as bad as some others who'd done it for different reasons. Yer don't get blamed. Yer blame yer'self. Some 'ow others come who've done some at like you and yer all feel that y'er want to do some at about it. It's a bit like being where y' are. You get together with others who 'av same interest as yer'self. We decided that th'only way we could do out about it was t' stop others doin' same. I can't tell yer 'ow long we've bin doing this but we're still doin' it. Y'e can see anybody y' want t'see any time. If I want see me mum an' dad, Elsie, Ada, our Raymond's first wife an' tons of others I only 'av to think of 'em.

People come to 'elp you in anything y' want to learn o' do. I can play piano now an' tons of other things I could never do when I was there. Anyway, for them that's asking, 'am sorry for what a did but am not much worse off than them who didn't do w'at I did. I can only speak for myself. I think there's others who did it for more selfish reasons than me an' 'av been told they're in a different place an' worse off than me. That's all I can really tell you. I tell you what. When you feel you've made up for everythin' it's a damn sight better 'ere than it was there. Don't do anythin' daft like I did. You'll come 'ere soon enough. Make best of yer time while you're there. Don't run away from anythin'. You'll only 'ave to make up for it when you come 'ere. Tell them who feel like I did not to do it. It's not worth it. Nothin' changes. You've to carry on from where you left off. You don't go to heaven an' you don't go to 'ell. You come 'ere an' it's not bad. Tell our Raymond, I met that lad Ken. 'es alright but 'e's not where I am. Tara!(Harold)

We have tried to write this answer in the same manner as it was transmitted by the father. None of us here have sufficient literary skill to transcribe the true accent in the way it deserves to be written. I doubt even if Myers has it. (Oliver)

QUESTION 10. You have mentioned the fact that light exists in the spirit world. Can you explain how this can be without a sun?

ANSWER. It was once suggested by a great teacher that you should let your light shine so that all may see your good works. Without meaning to be facetious, I am sure that you realise this teacher did not refer to a physical light, but rather the light of your mind and spirit. It was not suggested that you carry a candle or torch. Your question is best answered by reference to dreaming. I am sure that you will agree that most people sleep when it is dark, yet their dreams seem to take place in light-the light of the mind. Just as your physical sun causes a vibration within the ether called light, your awareness of it only takes place when that light hits some part of matter, for light itself is invisible to the physical eye. The world of the mind and spirit is full of etheric vibrations much higher than those of your light, therefore the mind world is full of light-brighter with each level of consciousness. The spirit world which is in a higher vibratory state than the mind world is of course brighter still. That is why sometimes you are able to be aware of the presence of some invisible friend. They bring with them the light of their own level of consciousness, enabling you to see them when earth is in either a state of light or darkness. In very low levels of consciousness there is very little etheric light. The intensity of etheric light is in accordance with the level of mind or spirit. (Phillipe)

QUESTION. 11. In the first book Oliver left the question of individuality unanswered. Do all human beings retain individuality?

ANSWER. Those who deserve to retain it do so. In answering your question, I am aware that your mind would suggest that some of the higher species of the animal world seem more human than those in your world and would seem more deserving of individuality than some of mankind. We have explained that we have no knowledge of what conditions

76

lie beyond our seven spheres, for our minds are not capable yet of understanding all the mysteries and secrets of creation. I understand that there is a level of semi-individualised mind, into which lower human mind passes together with that higher animal mind which is ready for human incarnation. Those who have come from this level and made no progress, have to return to it. Although you may have well earned your individualisation, whether you return to the level from whence you came depends on the progress you have made in your present incarnation. One could summarise this by saying that although there is no retrogression, there is statisticity. Remember that the mind consists of infinite levels and although the animals to which you refer may seem to have greater emotion and understanding than many humans, their intellectual, reasoning and other levels of mind may well be lower than those of human friends. The deciding factor would depend on the totality of mind development rather than certain aspects of mind. To use one of your familiar expressions-" Everyone gets what they deserve". If they deserve individuality, they get it. If not, they go into the same level as those minds rising from the animal kingdom to their first human incarnation. (Charles).

I feel that for those who have- read on-the questions dealt with have given sufficient stimulation of mind for the moment. We will continue to transmit our thoughts in further chapters then return later to deal with other questions that have, are being, and will be asked.

(The group)

CHAPTER 8

"LOVE IS A MANY SPLENDOURED THING"

I love that piece of music. I love that picture. I love to be in the country. I love to read. I love the colour blue.

I could continue in the above vane, but the examples given are sufficient to illustrate the fact that love does not necessitate the genders of male and female, for that music, picture, colour or countryside does not need a sexual label. Love is a common word in any language, yet it is not understood. In previous chapters, friends have used the term infinity, but who can claim a complete understanding of it. It would seem that love also has as many levels as the 'infinite' levels of consciousness in our spheres. The mother 'loves' her young whether they be male or female. Should I have used the word protects instead of love? Does the man who claims to love his wife really love her, or is it the fact that she provides his procreative instinct an opportunity to exercise itself. This equally applies to the woman who claims to love her man. How much of that which is claimed to be love is instinct? Here in this group we feel love for one another irrespective of whether the ethic duplicate demonstrates the male or female gender of our last incarnation.

I take this opportunity to express my feelings with regards to instincts, needs, protection, liking and love, yet respect the thoughts of others on these matters. Others in this group have referred to the beginnings of life on earth, when there was no necessity for male or female. The virus and amoeba manage to procreate without intercourse, as it is understood by mankind.

The bee-hive shows how it is possible for a community to work together for one purpose without any one wanting more than the other. The queen is their God. What a different world it would be if mankind could take example from the bee. Fish have a natural instinct to procreate so that eggs are laid. Many eggs are left by the mother who seemingly has little concern for their protection or survival. Some species of fish do seem to care for their offspring, demonstrating the emergence of the instinct of protection-the infancy of love. Birds lay eggs, nurture their young until they are able to leave the nest, then forget them. All animals have the instincts of procreation and protection. Some in lower levels of mind have several mates, whilst others have one. This surely illustrates that love, whatever it may be, is gradually passing from birth to infancy. The infinite levels of mind in mankind, part of the animal world, demonstrates the fact that love with some is very basic whilst with others it is a little more mature.

Some of the higher levels in our world show that love does no longer depend on genders of sex, for those minds have shed many bodies including the ethic. They have become spiritual light, with infinite levels of intensity, yet retain their individuality. This demonstrates that spiritual light can radiate a love far greater than when that light was confined to the physical and material earthly world. The necessity of male and female have then faded, yet love has become more real.

All these observations are made to remind those of you still wearing the robes of matter, that although the voice and body are used in an effort to express love, in actual fact, most are simply following the natural laws and instincts of procreation, need, desire, protection, yet still in the infancy of understanding love. It has been said that before you can love others you must learn to love yourself. I feel that it might have been better to say that before you can understand others it is necessary to understand yourself. " Man-know thyself". I suggest to you that understanding is but one of the many qualities that contribute towards pure love. Is it not true, that many have implicated in words and actions that their love is only for their wife or husband. " To thine own self-be true". Many who have uttered the words, " I love you" , have done so knowing that by so doing they have been able to satisfy their own wants, desires, instincts and passions. This is not true love. " Love thy neighbour as thyself". Who in the earthly world has sufficient understanding, empathy and concern for the welfare of others that they would lay down their life for another, other than their wife husband, son or daughter? Even the whales mourn the passing of their mate. Is mourning true love for the one who has returned home, or is mourning more often sympathy for oneself? We are still a long way from a true understanding of that word-LOVE-.

Many deceive themselves that by the acquisition of wealth and earthly treasures they will be able to be adored or loved by others. Look around you and see that those who are liked by others are those who have acquired knowledge, wisdom, spirituality, concern for others and a balance in giving and receiving. " Lay not up for yourselves treasures on earth where moth and rust doth corrupt, but rather lay up for yourselves treasures of the spirit-a better understanding of love".

It is unfortunate that many who hold religious offices and utter similar philosophies in their advice to others, do not follow their own advice. Often they utter the words of those great teachers of the past, hoping that they may be held in prestige, receive promotion and the admiration of those who listen. This applies in all religions. The ammunition of fear, ignorance and superstition are still being used instead of empathy, sympathy, understanding and love. The scientists who talk about the infinity of space should realise that love is also infinite and that their microscopes not only reveal the wonders of the world of matter but also the wonders of creation. Only then, will they learn to love God as well as appreciate the earthly world-one of the infinite nursery schools, where love is born. Doctors with their skill and knowledge may help to repair the damaged body, but the healing process is still a mystery to them. It is the love of God that heals. Once again, similar to those in religious offices, doctors also prefer self praise rather than admit that there are healing processes taking place that they are not able to explain.

Many of your modern songs include the word love, when in truth the words desire, lust and passion would be more appropriate. Even those who are beginning to understand that love is a greater thing than desire, sometimes forget to radiate their feelings towards other kingdoms of life. Not only the human kingdom responds to love, but other creatures within the animal world. The minds of those creatures who receive love will be helped to progress into a higher level from whence they came. Even plants and vegetables respond to care, thought and other qualities that constitute love. May I therefore plead with all who are reading this to extend their love beyond the human race. That other biblical philosophy, "Cast your bread upon the water and it will return to you a hundred fold", also-nay, more so applies to love. How can you expect to be loved if you never give it? How can you expect others to care for you if you only care for yourself?

I realise that in this chapter I have used many biblical quotations, for I realise that many readers still cling to the teachings of religious books of all creeds. May I therefore take the opportunity to express my opinion about these books. Their compilation has involved many of the thoughts of those teachers of the past. They also contain the added thoughts of those who collected the many scripts. If the words that are read are words that encourage love, then they belong to those teachers. The story of creation is not true word by word, for modern astronomers have shown how the earth was formed. There must have been an intelligence directing even this formation that included, " Let there be light" The biblical story telling how life gradually manifested in so many ways can be accepted if correct interpretation is given to it. It could well be that the ecclesiastics of those days long ago needed money or wanted it for either the church or themselves, therefore the saying that" It is easier for a camel to pass through the eye of a needle than a rich man to enter heaven" , may well have been added -not with love, but with greed. In your interpretation of all religious books, look for the philosophies that encourage the development of true love.

Turn back the pages of your own life to the chapters of youth. Many who read these pages would have to admit that great attraction was found in the opposite sex, so much so, that the words, " I love you" , could well have been used many times. Was it love, or was it the following of basic instincts? Without wishing to cause offence, is it true that' love' has reached its maximum with the wife or husband that you now have?

Some of you have experienced the loss of a husband or wife whom you felt could never be replaced, yet in some cases a greater 'love' has entered your life. The meaning of 'love', gradually changes, becomes more refined as you experience different relationships, therefore why should you presume that the partner you now have is the epitome of 'love'?

If reincarnation is a fact, then you have had many previous partners, whether you were incarnate as man or woman. Is your greatest 'love', to be found in your present incarnation, or in a previous one? Remember-you are on an infinite journey and on that journey you have incarnated many times. Every incarnation gives you the opportunity to find a finer meaning for that term 'love'. When physical incarnation is no longer necessary, you will continue to meet wonderful souls and realise that love is not confined to sexual gender. The 'love' that you shared with every person in every incarnation is never lost, but serves the purpose of helping you to reach a greater understanding of the term " love".

Do not feel from the thoughts expressed so far that we are recommending polygamy or celibacy. Polygamy is a human institution and incorporates those more basic instincts. It still exists in certain nations, but it will gradually disappear as those nations raise the standard of their environment and understanding. Without wishing to offend those nations, I suggest that polygamy is more to do with sensuality than 'love'. That infinite intelligence, God, did not only plan male and female for procreation, but so that mind could replace sensuality by affection. Mankind must therefore learn to have affection for one individual before he can learn to love his neighbour as himself. Monogamy is just one step towards that aim.

If all people were celibate then the human race would become extinct. This was never part of God's plan. Only if celibacy enables one to be of greater service to others, could it be considered as good. Celibacy is more often a selfish practice and a shirking away from social duty. The mother part of God-nature, suggests that it is natural for male and female to unite.

Previous chapters have made reference to the evolvement of mind through all the different kingdoms of life. The mineral kingdom only shows mind in its elemental stage-law and order, whereas the plant and vegetable kingdom shows the inclusion of vitality, or if you prefer-life, with all the parts of mind necessary to sustain it. The higher branches of the animal kingdom show the infancy of 'love', but still only in the form of need, protection, propagation, passion and desire. Mankind, being part of that kingdom cannot claim to have embraced every facet of 'love'. Love continues to become even greater in our worlds. Moving from one level of consciousness to another raises the vibrations of love. Do not ask about the condition of love outside those seven spheres for we only know what lies within them. It would seem an intelligent presumption, that if space is infinite, knowledge, experience, intelligence, wisdom, spirituality and " love" can also be infinite. To all who are willing to listen and -read on, we say with great sincerity, -" We love you".

(THE GROUP).

Phillippe
Real name Armand Marie Jacques Chastenet

CHAPTER 9

"FEELINGS"

Bon Soir. Je m'appelle Phillipe. My name in living life was not " Phillippe but since the name of one of the sons of this medium approximates to mine, I thought that Phillippe would be easier to remember. Es mon nom Importante? Is my name important-surely only to establish my identity during the time I was suffocated by earthly flesh and conditions. The reason for both Franz and I drawing close to this earthly friend, is his interest in the power of the mind and the use of that power for the welfare of both himself and others. " Physician-heal thyself". I am sure that Oliver has explained that in using Raymond we use his knowledge, his experience and add to it, transmissions of thought from ourselves. The biblical quotation that I have just used was taken from Raymond's mind, but useful since I would like to produce a cocktail of thought with regards to the use of hypnosis in healing as well as try to add to Oliver's thoughts on communication in our world.

There is nothing irreverent in suggesting that hypnotism has been used throughout the ages as a method of healing-even in suggesting that Jesus made great use of it, in producing what others called miracles. He even warned those around him to beware of those who might use this mysterious phenomenon for their own benefit. " For false Christs and false prophets shall rise and shall show signs and wonders, to seduce, if it were possible, even the elect".

The power of suggestion has been used and is still today used in nearly every walk of life-maybe that expression' walk of life' should now be changed to 'Run of life', in your modern world. By this expression I refer especially to politics and religion for is it not true that every political party and every religion suggest to people that their philosophy is the correct one? Your every day life is also bombarded by suggestions, that a certain vehicle, product or insurance is the best. This strange force has been used time and time again, sometimes by design, accident and often for deceit. Even ancient man was aware of this power although he, in his lack of understanding, would attribute it to superstitious origins. Many healers of the past suggested that all disease was due to evil spirits and by commanding those spirits to depart, many remarkable and miraculous cures took place.

It was myself who continued experimenting with' animal magnetism' after the death of Franz. My experiments proved that the mind seemed more efficient in the somnambulistic state than in waking state. Many of my

84

subjects, in what today you would call a deep hypnotic state, knew what I was tasting and even thinking, therefore the reality of telepathy became obvious to me long before Oliver's friend Myers did his experiments. Some claimed that they became aware of people who had died; they either saw a vision or heard voices. We had mediums before your Spiritualist movement began, and many of those mediums used to use a private mesmerist to enhance their mediumship. Descriptions of the spirit spheres were often given by those in a state of hypnotic entrancement. The medical profession of my day became very annoyed when they heard that often entranced subjects could diagnose their own disease and even suggest a cure.

It is not my intention to suggest that all mediums of today should use hypnosis, but to remind you that the power of suggestion may be put to better use than deceiving you that this, that or the other is the best. Even within your Spiritualism, is it not true that many sensitives have suggested that something will occur in the future, whether it be a move of house, marriage, or other prediction. Not all are given the gift of prophesy and many sensitives unconsciously or consciously suggest these things. The mind is so susceptible that it may put some of those suggestions into practice, feeling that it was meant to be and that the information or prediction came from the 'Spirit World'.

I do feel that some of our experiments could be repeated to prove to those of sceptical mind that telepathy is a reality. This would be one small step towards the acceptance that not only incarnate mind can communicate telepathically, but it might also encourage further experimentation into the possibility of communication from discarnate minds. Without repeating what some of my friends here have said, I would like to emphasise the fact that mind is infinite in its expansion. When incarnate as male one has the opportunity to develop the more earthly and scientific regions of mind, such as logic, reasoning, whilst when incarnate as female, the more delicate qualities of mind, such as intuition and emotion are exercised. This surely accounts for the fact that there seem to be more female mediums than male. Often, male sensitives and mediums would appear to be effeminate. They may have brought some of those female qualities of mind from a previous incarnation. Some who are incarnate as female, similarly display masculine qualities for the same reason.

In the case of Raymond, it is my pleasure and mission to help him in his hypnotic healing as well as inject some of those more delicate female qualities of mind into his mind during the trance state. I am sure he is always very pleased when I withdraw those qualities.

There is a strong relationship between the hypnotic state and dreaming, for it is related that a gendarme who assisted in an execution then

85

dreamed of being guillotined, afterwards committed suicide. Some dreams then, can have a very suggestive effect upon living life. Ordinary sleep is in my opinion an intermediate stage in-between the waking state and the deep hypnotic trance. Oliver has referred to the dream tunnel and suggested that there are infinite levels in the dream world. I agree. In that lower end of the dream state, memories are associated with physical life , whilst at the far end of that dream tunnel memories of the deeper or unconscious mind stimulate the dream story. These memories can include experiences of a previous incarnation, the totality of one's spiritual development, as well as telepathic transmissions from spiritual friends. Often problems may be solved, in the higher dream state, that could not be solved in the waking state. It is interesting to note that only the higher forms of life in the animal kingdom dream; even those who have not reached individuality dream as a rehearsal for the time when dreaming may serve a more useful purpose, as it does in the mankind. Having said this, it should also be remembered that some animals do retain individuality for a period of time. They too can transmit feelings to those they left behind, whether they be other animals or man.

Another interesting observation can be seen in the closeness of mind in identical twins. It is well known that they often feel the same joy or pain at the same time, and can communicate telepathically. Because of this, even when one dies, the other claims to feel their presence and guidance. This is at least a suggestion that a physical brain is not necessary for telepathic communication. The brain is only necessary for the received thought to be expressed in some physical manner. Not all of you are an identical twin and therefore, for you to receive good communication from our world to yours it is necessary to have a spiritual identical twin, as Franz is to Raymond.

I suggest to you that those musicians, in your earthly world, who are able to reach the pinnacle of the dream world are more able to be influenced by the minds of musicians who dwell in our worlds. The same could be said for scientists and all other forms of art. It is also true that lower minds in our worlds may travel down that same tunnel to meet and influence lower incarnate minds. That is why, in one of the previous chapters, Oliver said, " Dream well". The top end of the dream world is the entrance to the mind and spiritual worlds. You live in two worlds at the same time-the planetary life on earth and a cosmic life in one of our infinite levels of mind or spirit. It is necessary for the soul to withdraw from the physical for many reasons. First, to bring back replenishment to the physical body and secondly to remind the real self of its permanent abode. Friends here have described earthly conditions as a nursery school of God. In that sense it is true, for the mind and spirit needs the education that only manifestation in the world of matter can provide. If you think that your nursery school is the real world then what a shock you will have when you enter the infant school of mind, and even more so the university of spirit. Only when you have obtained your spiritual degree in that spiritual university will you be able to sit for your celestial masters diploma. I am still studying.

If the thoughts that I have just transmitted are true, -that the soul, mind or spirit withdraws or goes out of coincidence with the physical body during sleep, might this not also be true in the case of hypnosis? In the same way as the content of dreams can have an effect on one's way of life, hypnotic suggestion may also achieve the same result. It is also interesting to note that during ordinary sleep a subject may awaken easily if disturbed by a noise or pin prick, but the subject in deep hypnotic state can remain unperturbed by such events. This suggests that the spirit is further away from the physical during hypnosis than in ordinary sleep. This being so, it should be more possible for a hypnotic subject to achieve distant travelling than a person who is just asleep.

Although hypnosis may be used in what you today call hypno-therapy, I suggest that greater research should be carried out with regards to its use in psychical experiences-even for the development of mediumship. If it is possible for a subject to become aware of the hypnotist's thoughts and sensations telepathically, then it should be possible for the subject to become equally aware of external thoughts-thoughts from our worlds. We have been working closely with our friend Raymond, encouraging him to conduct experiments of this kind, and it may be of interest to those of you who are still reading to enumerate some of his cases.

A lady medium who was visiting said that she had a friend who was demonstrating mediumship in another country. By the use of hypnosis she was able to travel to that other country and see the place in which her friend was working. When she eventually met that friend, it was verified that what she had seen in her spiritual journey was true.

Raymond was working with another friend, at a time when one of his sons was on his honeymoon. The hypnotic subject was able to travel to the house of the son, and described how the son was sat on a bed, taking off his shoes and dressed only in his trousers. The following day, Raymond's son verified that what the hypnotised subject saw, actually did take place. Raymond's son said that he was glad that the experiment was not done a little later, for it would have been embarrassing.

A lady, attending a Spiritualist college, where many mediums were working came to Raymond expressing a desire to communicate with her departed mother. The lady was helped to reach an altered state of consciousness in which she was able to become aware of her mother's presence.

These related experiments help to suggest that hypnosis is a useful tool for sublime experiences that cannot ordinarily be achieved in consciousness, when the five physical senses are active. Many mediums suggest to people that they have a certain spiritual friend who helps to guide them during their earthly life. Would it not be better for you to be helped to personally become aware of that spiritual friend rather than accept the words of another, no matter how good a medium they may be. Those who engage themselves in the research of extra sensory perception would find that often hypnotised subjects would obtain a better score than those who were just relaxed. We in our world do not know all the answers, but gather around those who are willing both to listen and continue the interest that we had when in earthly conditions. I hesitate to mention the topic of regression in connection with hypnosis, yet regression does not only apply to previous lives, but to the life that you are now living. The fact remains, that if it be true that you have not only had one earthly incarnation, it should be possible , in some cases to have a glimpse of another. Surely, you are what you are today as a result of the total evolution of your mind and spirit. Oliver has stated that the mind has evolved through the mineral, plant and vegetable, animal and now human kingdoms of life. You must ask yourselves whether one human incarnation is sufficient to learn all the lessons of humanity, before continuing on your infinite spiritual journey. Should you fail to learn certain lessons in one of your earthly schools, you often have to stay another period of time in the same class. Why should this not be so with the lessons of the spirit? In whatever level of consciousness we dwell in our worlds, we cannot progress to the next level until we have exhausted the experiences provided in our present level.

I am not suggesting that the hypnotic state can guarantee a glimpse of a previous life, for often the mind can unconsciously invent a life, based on all that has been read and experienced in the present life. The fact remains, that some have been able to have experiences that can not be explained by crytomnesia. When we are able to speak our thoughts through this medium, many of you ask us about reincarnation, presuming that" death" gives the answer to this question and many other mysteries of life. Oliver has already stated that each one of us in this group can only say, " I am" , meaning that we still exist. It is natural that you should presume that we now know of all previous lives, but this is not so-at least, not yet. Oliver, when living, demonstrated the fact that he could not even remember many incidents of that life. We have agreed that a time may come on our journey, when we realise that no further progress may be made unless we return to earth's nursery school. I feel sure that free will exists in all levels here and that reincarnation necessitates a personal decision and desire. Our teacher, whom you are sometimes privileged to hear would say to us that reincarnation is an intelligent and logical process within creation. He is certainly wiser and more spiritual than we are. Shall we believe him? Do you believe us?

My name in living life was Armand Jacque Marie Chasenet and I was a student of Franz. Both Oliver and his friend Charles were both very interested in the phenomenon of hypnosis. Others in this group are equally enthusiastic in its use for showing the difference between brain and mind, as well as using it to benefit body, mind and spirit of our earthly friends. It is not surprising that we gather around our friend Raymond, for I understand you have an English expression, -" Birds of a feather flock together". The philosophy of this expression is more true in our worlds than it is in yours, for one of earth's lessons is the learning to live amongst and be aware of the different levels that prevail in earth's nursery school.

Communication of mind to mind is not limited to thoughts from our worlds to yours, for there are many examples of thoughts passed from one earthly person to another. Visions of living people may also be seen. Experiments in the past have shown that the minds of a group of friends sitting at a ouija board may be influenced by another living friend. Oliver tells us of when a lady was apported into the seance room, which suggests the process of de materialisation and re materialisation is not limited to the phenomenon known as materialisation from our worlds to yours. Telekinesis is another phenomenon that living people can sometimes demonstrate, when they move small objects with mind power. Your Spiritualism seems to want always to say that these various phenomena are always due to intervention from our worlds. It would seem to me that study of attempted communication of living to living would provide sufficient primary stimuli for the scientific community to investigate possible communication from our worlds to yours. We do not understand why your many religions say that communication from living to living is telepathic, but from living to dead is evil. Until recently your scientific communities have shied away from anything that cannot be measured or repeatedly tested. We are aware that they talk of parallel universes, but seem unwilling to accept the fact that intelligences exist in those universes. Instead of researching those who claim to have out of the body experiences, many would rather attribute them to imagination or hallucination.

With greater understanding of all these matters it would seem common sense to use super extra sensory perception, or better still mediumship, to communicate with those lying in comatose condition and those who are possibly having what is termed out of the body experience. The bodily functions may be incapable of expressing communication but the mind is quite capable. In my living days, we did not have the knowledge or experience to attempt these things, but now, even with your advanced technology, it would appear that you would rather apply it to more material matters.

Not all death bed visions limit themselves to people who have 'died'. Often a person on their death bed will claim to see a person, who they think is still living. Because of the circumstances, nobody told them that the living person actually died a few days ago. This being so, it cannot be said that death bed visions are either imagination or a natural instinct built into the brain to give a calming effect during the final moments of life. If it be true that people see visions either prior to death or even in healthy state, then it cannot be true that we all have to lie buried until the day of the great resurrection. I didn't-I'm here.

Oliver has mentioned the fact that time does not seem to matter in the dream state, and he has also drawn a parallel between the higher dream state and existence in our worlds. In the sense that time does not exist in our worlds and that communication is telepathic, he is correct. In referring to a dream tunnel, he may have suggested to you that our world is like dreaming. You must remember that many who set off on a journey to one of our levels, do not believe that there is anywhere to go after death. They, therefore feel that they are dreaming. They are, and will continue to stay in that dream world until their minds accept the fact that, at the end of that dream tunnel is a more real world than the one in which they lived on earth. Rescue circles show that there are many souls who do not believe that they have died. These poor souls have hardly entered the dream tunnel. The minds of many are so closed, that they feel they are in darkness. They cannot even hear the thoughts of those who want to help them. A complete understanding of birth, life and death will enable you to pass through that dream tunnel so fast, that it will seem to you that you have at last returned to the real world.

Although it is true, that many friends will be there to welcome you back to that real world, it is also true that not every friend or relation can be there. You must remember that some of your friends have found their place in a lower level of consciousness than yours. You will of course be able to visit them. As soon as your mind desires to see them, experienced friends will take you to the level in which your friends dwell.

I feel that I have transmitted the thoughts that I felt important. The friends gathered around me feel that there is more to be understood from the answers that we try to give to your many questions. The next chapter will be devoted to answering some of those questions. Mercy beaucoup for reading my thoughts. I will still be helping in the group as we now move on to those answers to your questions. I hope that we are able to give some sense and satisfaction to some, if not to all. Please remember as you read the answers, that sometimes these answers may differ from your present opinion. It is not our intention to change that opinion, but only to provide food for thought. At one time, all thought that the earth was flat. I'm sure that the discoveries of those astronomers who proved the earth to be a sphere, hurt the minds of many. The truth often hurts. In the following chapter, I pray that the pain is not too severe.

(PHILLIPPE).

MIDFACE

I must confess that in reading the pages written so far, I have found many answers, yet I am still not satisfied. I still yearn for some indisputable proof of life after death. Many times when day dreaming, I am taken to a book, -even to a certain page. There I find some information relevant to one of my enquiries. Even objects that my wife and I misplace, are found by asking. It may sound incredible to readers, but it really works. Many times I refuse when my wife says, "Ask Oliver and your friends where it is". I stubbornly say, "No, I cannot rely on my friends to do everything for me". I continue to look for hours then, in the end ask. A thought where to go, comes into my head and the lost object is found. I suppose this is just one way my invisible friends help to convince me that they are really around. Cryptaesthesia may be the answer for objects that I have misplaced, but not for those that my wife has lost. If I have access to my wife's mind then at least it proves the reality of telepathy. It is more than that. I hear the thought in my mind.

The other day, when we had some guests, the receiver on the satellite receiver started to change channels at an alarming speed. My wife said that it was a sign that Oliver or one of my friends wanted me to sit. I did sit for those friends and it was confirmed that the phenomenon was a sign that this sitting should take place. At other times one light in the room will blink. I suggest to my wife that it is just a change over of generators in the Spanish grid system, but since only one light blinks, she refuses to accept my explanation and I have to sit for trance. Invariably my wife is correct. Often, I joke, telling her that I feel like one of our dogs when she gives the command, -"SIT"

Having just finished the chapter on questions and answers, I realise that some of the earlier chapters written by various spirit friends, have been written in answer to some of my own mental enquiries. Maybe there is some truth in that biblical saying, "Ask and you shall receive".

At this moment in time I am just preparing to go on a third tour in order to help promote the first book. This second book is half finished and the thought came into my head-If there is such a thing as a preface, why shouldn't there be a middle face. Maybe there will be an end face also. I have quickly read parts of some of the proceeding chapters, and like the mediums Oliver talked about, I too wonder from where all the information and thoughts come. Are they coming from my own sub-conscious, or they truly coming from Oliver and his friends? Up to now, I feel that it is a mixture of both, but even saying that, I realise the fact, that I am half admitting their existence. Maybe the doubt within my mind is gradually subsiding.

I'm sure that one of us has mentioned that I have to listen to tapes of what has been said, or listen to my wife relating what has taken place during a session. My wife, June has much more confidence in my friends than I do. These days, one of the invisible friends speak to her every morning after I have drunk my morning tea. She takes longer to drink hers than I do, and whilst I am waiting, I seem to drift off into that altered state in which my friends can use me. The way June talks to Oliver makes me think that he has seven daughters instead of only six, for she talks to him as if he were her father.

As well as the trance condition, I am still doing hypno- therapy and have noticed a difference in it. These days, it seems as if I get a lot of help. I never need to give any thought to how I am going to work with any patient. Thoughts seem to come naturally, and Phillippe claims that he and Franz are always very close when I am working. The other day, a lady came for regression. She said that she had tried hypnosis three times before and it had never worked. In the session that we had together she managed to get a glimpse of one of her previous lives—or was it just her wild imagination? Either way, the lady seemed quite satisfied with the results and naturally wants to come again.

Since the trance condition came, I have noticed that June and I have become unnaturally telepathic. I say unnaturally because I am aware that many husbands and wives often feel one another's thoughts. June and I have nearly reached a stage when neither of us need speak. We behave more like identical twins. She says that when she talks with our invisible friends in a morning, they too very often-no-more than very often, speak of things that she is thinking about at that moment.

We enjoyed the last tour, although the motor home in which we travelled only just managed to get us home, due to my lack of knowledge of it's proper requirements in servicing. June tells me that in some churches people came hoping to get a message from their loved ones. Maybe they were not informed that my trance state is not for that purpose. ——"There are divers gifts". Even as I try to write my own thoughts in this mid-face, I can hear odd thoughts coming into my mind, like the italicised expression that I have just used. With my close friends, I often joke saying that if there is no spirit world, I'm staying here, for I have not yet completely rid myself of the fear of dying. Only the complete knowledge that there is somewhere to go, will take that fear away.

I often feel hypocritical for the sessions of trance or regression that we do, seem to give other people more assurance of the existence of that spirit world. As for myself, I cannot say that I have knowledge of a previous life, although I seem to have a deep inner feeling that I once was a member of a monastery.

In Psychic News and Psychic World I read about the work of many healers in different countries and of their miraculous cures. I am very pleased for those who benefit from such healing yet at the same time, have to bear in mind some of the words written by the group. I think it was Phillippe who suggested that even Jesus may have had his failures in healing and I am sure that this applies to all healers. Recently June and I have been helping a Spanish lady, who heals using stones and sea water. Without doubt, her ability to diagnose is beyond belief, and many of her patients respond to her healing ability. People come from England to see her and we are fortunate to hear the results of the Spanish lady's healing work, for we often receive telephone calls from those who have been to see her. Sometimes we feel that we witness a miracle, for many respond immediately to her work, whilst at other times we feel sad when we are told that some have died. My wife continues with her healing and I am able to see similar results. More often than not, patients come both to June and the Spanish lady, when they are in their last few weeks of earthly life, hoping for that miracle. Even though not all respond physically, I have to conclude that all are helped in some way or other, for the healing work in both cases, prepares them for that inevitable journey that we must all take. It seems that all healers must accept some physical failures in healing, but are consoled by the fact that Spiritual success is nearly always achieved. It is therefore always nice to read of successes in healing, but we must not run away with the idea that all are cured physically.

I often think about the friends who no longer dwell on earth-my first wife, our mothers and fathers, together with others with whom we either worked or played. Have they really missed very much since their passing? Life for most of us here consists of concern about money, relationships and many other earthly matters. If the other world was all heaven, then by comparison, conditions on earth would, to some, feel like hell. Maybe some doubt is necessary. If we were all sure of those other worlds, some of us might want to make an early departure. That might help to explain why we are not born remembering where we came from. As my invisible friends suggest-sure knowledge of those other dimensions would take away the need for faith and hope.

Down here in Spain, the nights are often clear, enabling those who are interested, to look at the sky at night. I'm sure that many readers in this and other countries have, like myself, gazed in wonder at all the stars and other heavenly bodies. It would seem natural to conclude that life could not only exist on this one planet in this one galaxy. I wonder whether life forms in other parts of creation wonder about God and whether there is eternal life. Whatever forms of life there are, they must all feel that God is similar to themselves.

Oliver says that my body is like a motor car and that my mind or spirit is the driver. I feel that time has come for me once again to jump out of my motor car so that others may drive it. Talking of motor cars—;June and I have now done several tours in England. These were done at the suggestion of the publisher, so that people could see how the book came to be written. In order to do these tours we bought an American motor home so that we would not have to stay in hotels every night. During the first tour the gearbox ran short of oil and repairs cost nearly two thousand pounds. Since we are resident in Spain, we also had to pay for the number plates to be changed. This also costs allot of money. I only mention this so that readers may be assured that the tours and the selling of the book has certainly not been arranged for any financial gain.

In the preface I mentioned coincidence and the fact that Oliver said that there was no such thing. Those involved in Spiritualism will know that the tours have taken us to Liverpool, where Oliver was professor of physics in the university. The tours have also taken us to Birmingham, where he was principal of it's university and also very close to Normanton house, his last place of residence. We have, in a way traced Oliver's life story, for one of the tours included Fenton, a place very close to where Oliver was born. June and I were able to photograph the ground of the house in which he lived when principal of Birmingham university—"Mariemont", and also visit the actual house in which he died-(sorry—was reborn)—"Normanton house"-in Wilsford. It really seemed as if all this was arranged for us—by whom? In trying to find Normanton house, we stopped to ask a lady whether she knew of it's whereabouts. By ' coincidence' she happened to be connected with tourism and said that Normanton house was only two hundred yards down the road. I told her the reason why I wanted to see it and showed her Oliver's book. She said that it might not be wise to drive my motor home up the driveway as the owner might not appreciate it. On arriving at Normanton house, I had the feeling that it would be alright to drive straight up to the house. I knocked at the door and was met by a very hospitable gentleman. On telling him the reason for my visit and showing him the book, he invited us inside, showed us around, gave us tea and biscuits and was interested in my story. His charming wife and daughter joined us, saying that we were very welcome to have a good look around the house and grounds. It was a very emotional experience for I felt that I knew where the library used to be and how the house looked before extensions were added. I pointed to an large outside building, asking the owner whether the stables used to be there. They did. The delight of that visit came when my wife took a photograph of me standing near the house. Oliver has confirmed the fact that he influenced certain minds so that we could visit these places. If all that took place on those tours was coincidence then our lives must be full of 'coincidences' Very close to Normanton house lies the church where the memorials of Oliver, his wife and one of his daughters can be seen We were inspired to visit the churchyard where we found these memorials. The words on Oliver's and those on his wife's are worth quoting., for they make reference to their wonderful family and also to the research that Oliver did in an effort to prove survival, not only for his own satisfaction, but also as a comfort to those who were bereaved. I cannot describe the feelings in my mind as June and I stood in that churchyard looking at the following words inscribed on the walls of that church. We will treasure the photographs that we took. Perhaps after reading them you will be able to understand more why he has continued to try to transmit his thoughts on the same theme.

To the memory of
MARY F.A. LODGE
wife of Sir Oliver Lodge
and proud mother of
six sons and six daughters
a happy loving and devoted family
her time on earth lasted from
11 March 1851
To 20 February 1929
when she passed happily on
to rejoin some and
to await reunion with others.

ALSO

to the memory of her husband
OLIVER JOSEPH LODGE
born 12th June 1851
died 22nd August 1940
Thankful for the love which has
surrounded him throughout his
time on earth full of certainty
about continued existence
and hopeful that his writings may
be a comfort to the bereaved.

If my rambling in this mid-face seems to be rubbish, the following chapters might help to suggest that we can all at times be influenced by minds superior to our own. I do hope that the chapters written so far, have given as much hope to readers as they have given to me. Here come my invisible friends. For now-cheers. Hope to see you somewhere—sometime.

RAY.

Ray Smith at Normanton House

CHAPTER 10

"FOR ALL WE KNOW"

As the song title suggests, we take the opportunity to relay some of the questions that we have been privileged to try to answer, hoping that one of them may be one of yours-one who is willing to read on. Some of the following questions merit an answer that virtually requires a chapter. However we will attempt to give our answers in as clear and concise manner as possible.

QUESTION. 1. I understand some of the things you have said about the difficulties in communication. How can I be sure that the information given to me by mediums comes from the spirit world?

ANSWER. It is very difficult to be sure. In previous writings I mentioned the fact that in my sittings with Mrs. Piper, Mrs. Leonard and other mediums I seemed to receive evidence of the continued survival of my friend Myers, my son Raymond, my aunt Anne as well as many other friends. At the same time, in a previous chapter, I said that much information could be obtained unconsciously by mediums from the energy fields and auras of sitters. We have also stated that most mediums are not sure themselves from where the information that they receive comes. How can you be sure that the words that you read, originate in the minds of the group assembled here rather than in the mind of Raymond? It must be admitted that evidence given by mediums often comes in symbolic form, or in bits and pieces. You must ask yourself why Myers informed me, of the death of my son Raymond, in mythological terms instead of saying, " I'm sorry to inform you that——". As mentioned previously, I left seven envelopes, one inside the other, with the society, hoping that some medium would be able to convey the contents of the inner envelope. One sensitive saw a picture of the main statement whilst others mentioned parts of it's content. I even left a message that the final envelope could be psychometrised. From what I have already written and spoken, you can see that my attempt was futile. In any case, the question of survival should not be based upon one sitting with a medium, but rather on a series of experiments. With this medium Raymond, you must sit many times with him, so that you may assess whether the thoughts received could all come from his mind.

Whether it be automatic writing or trance utterances, I can now assure you that there is always a certain amount, if not a lot of dilution, by the medium concerned. A few memorised facts do not give proof of an individual mind. Only a building up of evidence through many sittings and experiences with all forms of mediumship, will help to give the conviction that you seek. I have previously said that some sittings with Mrs. Piper suggested that her spirit friend was 'fishing', for facts. Other sittings gave evidence. Another medium, Mrs. Willett gave great classical knowledge which could only have come from my friend Myers. I ought to mention that I am now in a position to verify this. The cross correspondences have given the greatest evidence so far, but how many spiritualists have taken the trouble and patience to study them? Like sheep they continue to flock to their churches hoping that one day, their loved ones will find some medium who can relay their actual words. Nobody wants to listen-and yet the fact remains that communication from our worlds to yours is telepathic-rather like communication in dreams. If some medium happens to give you a correct name or fact, how can you be sure that they have not obtained it from some living mind? Super extra sensory perception may explain many of the facts relayed by mediums but it will not explain how skills, habits, mannerisms, turns of phrase and other aspects of personality are received by sensitives and mediums. This medium never knew me, nor anything about me or my friends here, yet we seem to be able to have him feel our personalities. We have to rely on the tools of his mind to transmit scientific or medical knowledge and are lucky if he manages to transcribe our thoughts in the words of our desire.

The information that astronomists have been able to collect with regards to that part of the universe within range of their instruments, is less than one drop of water within all oceans when compared to an understanding of all creation. In similar fashion, the amount of collected evidence for survival gathered so far is not sufficient to even whisper, " We survive". In previous discussions it has been asked, " If we have truly lived previous lives, why can we not clearly remember them, for this would give personal evidence of a spirit world". We have used expressions like" drinking the cup of forgetfulness" , in order to give some understanding of this but realise that expression, although true, is not sufficient. If you could bring all memory into each incarnation, you might realise that there are greater loves here in our worlds than you have found in your present incarnation. There are more wonderful experiences to be had in our worlds than any presented in earthly life. However there are certain experiences that only earthly life can give. If one had complete cognisance of all lives, it would not allow one to fulfil the true purpose of one's present earthly incarnation.

It could also be argued that complete conviction of survival would take away the necessity for faith or hope. The knowledge that life never ends might take away the desire to complete the task of' 'living'-the purpose of earthly incarnation. The struggle for gaining knowledge with regards to birth, life and death is all part of this purpose. In further answer to your question it must also be said that decades ago, when the Society for psychical research was formed, there were sufficient members with sufficient funds, time and interest for progress to be made in pursuing the question of survival. Today, there may be many wealthy people with sufficient time to devote to these matters, but it would seem for the moment that they would rather devote their money and energy to the pursuit of more physical, sensual and earthly pleasures. The pendulum will one day swing and when it does, neuroscientists, physicists, theologians and others with intellectual capacity will combine their knowledge. In so doing they will draw a little closer to proving that there are intelligences and forces outside the realms of matter. Thank you for your question and allowing us to give our thoughts on survival.

QUESTION. 2. Is it possible for a person in this western world to be reincarnated in some under-developed society.

ANSWER. I do not wish to sound facetious, but your question rather depends upon your definition of developed. Your western world may be more advanced in it's technology and material assets. Ask yourself whether it is more advanced in it's spiritual values. We have in previous writings encouraged you to differentiate between knowledge, experience, intelligence, wisdom and spirituality. Many in the western world have the first three qualities, but lack wisdom and spirituality. The" Old wise man of the mountains" , may not have had a university education yet many would prefer to take his advice rather than that of some university professor.

With regards to a direct answer to your question, it is possible for one from more materially developed countries to reincarnate in a country that is less materially advanced. Opportunities to develop spiritual values may well be greater in what you call an under-developed society, therefore those who realise this, may choose to take that opportunity. Similarly, it is possible for one who has great wisdom and spirituality, to reincarnate in your western world. They would do so in an effort to influence mankind that earthly treasures are of no use in our worlds. Only spiritual qualities enable one to progress from one level of mind to a higher one.

The challenges of physical life not only involve various zodiac signs, the inherited genes, but also colours of skin, different religious thoughts as well as experience in different cultures. Do not presume then that the western world is the perfection of man's earthly experiences. Some lessons may only be learned in what you have called under developed countries. May we take this opportunity to remind you that Indian tribes of the past, gave thanks to the buffalo before consuming it's meat. Some countries in your western world do not pay sufficient respect to lower forms of life, even though spirit manifests in them. Your soul, spirit and mind has used those lower manifestations of life to progress to a stage when it may retain it's individuality. Once again, we implore you not to make judgement on the material aspects of life but rather on spiritual values. (Group)

QUESTION. 3. Where is the spirit world?

ANSWER. It is everywhere. I realise this statement needs greater clarification, therefore with your patience we will try to explain. As we have said many times, your physical world is limited in many ways, particularly by time, distance and speed. Those who dwell in the mental and higher spheres of our worlds do not have these limitations. The etheric vibrations have certain limitations, such as the speed of light, but the individual who has shed the etheric body, may be instantaneously where the mind wishes to be. Just as your physical sun shines on many parts of your earth at the same time, so those who dwell in spheres outside etheric limitations may be in several places at the same moment. Those who dwell in higher mental and celestial spheres, manifest as non-physical light that can be felt in all levels of consciousness of lower spheres. The spiritual radiation of great teachers of the past can be felt by many on earth at the same time, no matter in which hemisphere their country lies. You only become aware of those spiritual transmissions that match your receiving frequency. In order to receive thoughts from any higher frequency than your own some intermediate frequency must be used. In simpler terms, those who dwell in sphere six may receive thoughts from sphere seven and pass them down to sphere five. Even then, it depends on whether or not those in sphere five are capable of understanding higher thoughts.

To return to the location of our worlds, many in orthodox religions, no doubt feel that God resides or manifests in church-God's house. Those who attend Spiritualist churches hope that their loved ones will be there and will be able to make their presence known through some medium. I wonder whether thought is given to where their loved one's go after the service is over? Those who now dwell in the invisible world are only a thought away, but whether you can know of their presence depends on several factors. Your materialistic world prohibits the possibility of many developing their standard of sensitivity and mediumship to a high enough degree, so that they may translate thoughts and symbolism into appropriate words. The sceptical and negative attitude of people often put up a barrier through which even the most developed mediums find it hard to penetrate.. Do not presume that your wife, son, daughter or friend dwells in the same level of mind as yourself. They may have to use some intermediate frequency of mind to even reach the mind of the medium or yourself. Even when they do so, remember that all communication is telepathic. Since your friends in our worlds no longer have a physical voice, they often have to use symbolism or sentience in their thought transmission. The astral, etheric, mind, spirit and celestial worlds are in a sense all part of your world, but in a different vibratory state. Air is that part of your atmosphere which is used to transmit sound. Although it is all around you, only one small part is used when you speak to someone. Without physical objects, you would not be aware of the lower etheric vibrations such as light, gravitation, magnetism, electricity and cohesion. It is these lower etheric vibrations that are used by those in our worlds to create physical phenomena. The mental, spiritual and celestial vibrations pervade the whole of creation. They are therefore always with you, but your friends who dwell in them, find it very hard to make you aware of their presence. To summarise, the spirit world is every-where-only a thought away. The dream world is only a dream away. Your dreams are often an expression of the mind in symbolic form, yet often contain a wealth of information. It will be my privilege and pleasure to transmit thoughts concerning the dream world in this second book-for those who are willing to read on. The mind and spirit world are at the far end of the dream world-in the invisible world-invisible to physical eyes, but visible to spiritual eyes. Maybe like the new born kitten, you have not yet learnt how to open your(spiritual)eyes. Thank you for your question.

QUESTION. 4. What is it like in the spirit world?

ANSWER. Wonderful. I have tried in previous chapters to give some idea of the conditions that prevail in our WORLDS. You will notice that I have emphasised WORLDS, for the conditions in every level of consciousness are different. Let me once again say that everything that exists in every level only exists because of the memories, experience and creative ability of the minds of those who dwell there. That is why you may hear many different stories. Unlike your earthly world of matter that is limited by it's shape and size, our worlds do not have those limitations, unless the mind requires them. You may well ask whether those who dwelt long ago in caves, before the time of houses, still dwell in caves, and if their level of mind be the same as yours, whether their cave would be next to your modern house. The old wise man of the mountain may be on the same level of mind as yourself but with his wisdom would not want to mentally place his cave next to your house. Remember, the mind is infinite in it's number of layers and that it's development depends on knowledge, experience, wisdom and spirituality. These qualities also embrace logic, intellect, emotion, sympathy, empathy, desire to progress, creative ability, individual feelings and infinitely more. One would hope that those who long ago once dwelt in caves had evolved through incarnations and learning, so that now they had no desire to live in a cave. Similarly, one would hope that one day you

102

would realise that an etheric duplicate of your modern house is no longer necessary. Those who still want to live in a cave may continue to do so along with others who have the same level of knowledge, intellect, wisdom, etc. -in other words, those who have the same mental qualities and desires dwell in the same level of consciousness. Since the spirit world contains an infinite number of these levels, I may only describe the conditions that prevail in the level in which I and my friends dwell.

My friends and I still enjoy the joys of the country; -trees, flowers, rivers streams, mountains , animals, birds, and many other features of nature that prevailed on earth when we were there. We all enjoyed the music of the masters. There are therefore musicians capable of playing that music. They obtain as much pleasure in playing as we do listening. The listeners are on the same level as the players. My friend Myers was a literary scholar. There are therefore libraries, universities as well as all other facilities for the desire of the artistic mind. I have a laboratory, as do many other scientifically minded inhabitants of this level. There are equal opportunities for those of both scientific and artistic interests just as there are in your world of matter.

To answer your question, the spirit world for you will consist of all the desires of your mind and spirit. You will share that level with others who have the same interests, desires, knowledge, wisdom and spirituality as yourself. At the moment, you may, through the restrictions of finance or whatever, be struggling to obtain your ideal living conditions. Here, in your deserved level of mind you may live where your mind dictates, finding that your companions are of like mind. If you and your companions do not desire to learn, there will be no places of learning. For those who desire the pursuit of more earthly pleasures, there will be those facilities available. Think for a moment of the different interests, likes, dislikes, abilities and passions of your earthly friends and acquaintances. This will suggest the reason why there are infinite levels of mind in the spirit world, and why it is impossible to describe them all in one simple answer.

Those who make money a god will have a plentiful supply of it. They will be with others who also worship money. One can create a mental simulation of any material object that one has experienced in the process of living. Knowledge, experience, wisdom and spirituality have to be gained by the progression of mind. Is not true that money is more appreciated when you have to work for it? Anything that is in abundant supply is not valued. Those who desire to pursue those more sordid pleasures of drink, sexual perversions and other gross interests will be with others of like mind. Gold is only valuable because there is less of it than soil. When drink, sexual pursuits and other morbid interests are freely available they also lose their value. There comes a desire to gain those things that one does not have-knowledge, wisdom and spirituality.

As I have said before, the heavenly music of my level may be hell to those who dwell in other levels-each to his own. Unlike earthly conditions where you have mixed levels of consciousness, in our worlds those of like mind find themselves on the same level.

Think then, of the desires of your own mind, and you will be able to visualise that level of consciousness in which you will after physical death, find yourself. I and my friends, as well as other groups in the same level want to share our experience and knowledge with others incarnate and discarnate. We enjoy having all the features of nature around us. They are here. We need universities, libraries, halls of learning, theatres, concert halls, laboratories, art studios, paintings, houses, golf courses, tennis courts, as well as many other facilities of work and play. In that sense conditions in our level are similar to those that prevailed in our earthly life, yet in a sense different. They appear just with a thought. They are better. The colours are brighter. The animals are not aggressive. Even the flowers seem to talk to us, as do all forms of life in our world.

This is hard to explain. In your world aggressiveness is born of fear or necessity of food. In our non physical world, food is not required and since we no longer clothe ourselves with a physical body, no creature can harm us. Other forms of life, other than human are there because of our desire and love for them. It is this love which makes them more peaceful and tranquil than those creatures that dwell on earth. Are not the domesticated pets that you have less aggressive than those that dwell in the wild. If the wild lion's stomach was full, and it was not afraid that you would harm it's young, I'm sure that it would not attack you.

I would hope that the conditions we describe seem those of your desire. If so, we will meet in the not too distant future. See then, that it is impossible to describe what it is like in the spirit world, for the conditions are infinite in their nature. The conditions that prevail in the animal world are different than those in the insect, fish, plant and bird world, yet all on the same planet. The conditions in every level of mind are similarly different, yet all in the same mind world. We therefore apologise if our answer does not satisfy your curiosity. Thank you for your question.

QUESTION. 5. If, as you say, when we die we all go to different levels of mind, how can I be with my wife, mother father and other friends?

ANSWER. You might have also asked how it is that I can be with my dog, cat, canary or other earthly friend no matter in what level of life they manifested. Although you may love your earthly wife, husband friend or even pet, that does not mean to say that you are on their level of consciousness, yet you all live happily together. Love-true love is like a magnetic force that bonds souls together. In earthly life, some of us were scientists, professors, or doctors. Our wives and friends were not. That did not mean that they were in a lower level of consciousness. We were able to spend much time together, yet able to pursue our various interests, work and play. So it is here. We in this group work together for a single purpose, but can meet our loved ones whenever our thoughts are directed towards them. The bond of love affords this amenity. You surely do not want to be with your dog, peacock, canary or even wife every moment of time. Love enables you to go to their level of mind. Possession is not love. Those for whom you have great love would want you to allow them to progress. They may only do this in their own level of mind, but may meet you whenever they or you desire. Your love for your cat, dog or peacock would encourage you to release them from their temporary individuality, so that they may continue their development of mind, and eventually make individuality permanent. Owning is not loving. If you really love your child, wife, dog, cat, peacock or canary, you would want it to have the same chances of progressing as you have. You do not like to be owned. Why should they? If once again, I may steal the title of a song from Raymond's memory store, I would change the words of " Please release me, let me go, for I don't love you anymore, to, " As you release me and let me go, I know of your very great love for me".

May we take this opportunity to remind you that you will not only meet the loves of your present life, but love that still persists from previous lives. I wonder which is the greater. You may have a very great surprise. Love in your present incarnation is very limited. Accept then that although you can be with your present loves any time you wish, you will also want to equally be with others.

(The group)

CHAPTER 11

DREAM "DREAM WHEN YOUR FELLING BLUE
THAT'S THE THING TO DO".

I have stated in previous writings that there is a greater parallel between our world and the dream world than there is between our world and your earthly world of matter. This statement is by no means sufficient, for the dream world deserves a treatise of it's own. Many books have been written concerning dreams and in them it has been suggested that when you dream of a certain object, animal or incident, it would have a certain meaning. Some of the mediums whom I was privileged to know, explained that a vision of a rose would have a special meaning for them. A rose for others meant something different. I suggest that dreams are similar in the fact that often they contain symbolism. A symbol for one person can mean something different for another.

I understand that just before the assassination of an American president, a lady dreamt of a black cloud over the White House. As the dream repeated itself, the cloud became both darker and lower. Obviously the dream had to be interpreted by the dreamer. Whether the origin of the dream came from the lady's sub conscious or from some spirit friend, it did not give specific details as to it's meaning. I can now confirm that this is the reason why my friend Myers was not able to communicate the actual words" Your son Raymond has been killed", but instead transmitted" You take the part of the poet and he will act as FAUNUS. " My knowledge of Latin enabled me to realise that this was a warning of some impending calamity. At the time I thought that it might be of a financial nature. Only when we received the telegram telling of Raymond's death, did I realise that the Faunus message was a warning from Myers, not from his physical conscious but rather from his sub-conscious-expressed in classical terms. For those who are still reading on-Myers was a great classical scholar. Only now do I understand why the message was expressed in this manner. Forgive me for digressing, but I feel the story just told is relative to dreaming, for dreams are more an expression of the sub or unconscious rather than the conscious. The language is different. Perhaps this might also help to explain why it is that we in our dimensions are able to communicate telepathically by all forms of art instead of words.

Let us continue our treatise on dreams. This will obviously need some reference to sleep, since dreams usually occur during the period of sleep. Not always, for there is such a state as day-dreaming. What is it then that occasions sleep. Maybe it is a saturation of the bodily organs including brain, by waste products accumulated during the day's activities? It cannot be said that a newly born baby needs sleep because of exhaustion through the day's activities. I can now positively state that a baby spends much of it's time in our worlds-if you prefer-astrally projected. Those who are fortunate or unfortunate to reach a very old age, also spend much of the full day asleep-in our worlds.

Here, reference could be made to that type of sleep induced by hypnosis, which often can give more benefit than that of spontaneous sleep. It is also true that during this hypnotic sleep many become more aware, become more sensitive to the reality of our worlds than they do in ordinary sleep. Is it not also true that through accidents or whatever some people pass from consciousness, through sub-consciousness to unconsciousness and on returning claim to have had very revealing experiences-some claiming to have become temporary aware of the mysteries and secrets of creation? Sleep then, rather than being a negative part of life is possibly more positive than the waking state. I have stated before that even a few moments of sleep can give greater regeneration than hours spent just resting. Why is this? Does the spirit really leave the body during the time of sleep, and if so, is this what regenerates the physical body enabling it to be more efficient when conscious? Yes. Some musical composers claim to have received their inspiration during sleep. Scientists also wake up finding a solution to a problem that they could not solve when awake. I am sure that those of you who are taking the trouble to read on, will admit that some of life's problems are solved during the sleep period. Have you not woken up, finding the answer to the problem which confounded you yesterday? Sleep then, deserves to be given as much consideration as waking time. The dreams that occur during sleep have a more profound effect on us than we ever realise, for they can be compared with a post-hypnotic suggestion, resulting in either joy, sadness, achievement or disillusionment. Dream well.

The dreams that take place during sleep give access to far greater memory than that available during the waking state. Memory during the waking state is generally limited to the thoughts that will be of use to the day's activities or those planned for the immediate future. The only memories necessary during the waking state are those which will help to make life less painful and provide some pleasure through the five physical senses. Dreaming does not involve these senses, therefore memory is more free to expand, to include not only experiences of the present incarnation, but also include memories from others. I am sure that you have heard your friends sometimes relate the fact that they had a strange dream. It was only strange when compared to activities involved in the waking part of the day.

Some of the higher manifestations of life other than man, also seem to dream. Observe your dog. Whatever be the purpose of dreaming, it not only applies to mankind but also to other forms of life. Does a worm need to dream? Does a virus? As I read the mind of this medium, I see that he has dreamt of being able to play the trumpet far better than he ever could in any part of his present living life. Although in his youth, I understand that he could play very well, the dream state presented him with the opportunity to play as his mind desired, without the hindrance of the limitations of his earthly body. Actually, he often plays for us in his dream state, but cannot bring memory of it back when he awakens. If you could all have vivid recall of your experiences during sleep period, you would not want to return to consciousness. You might not even want to continue with living life. That is why you forget. The dreams that you remember, serve a useful purpose in your waking state, even though they may have been symbolic. They are dreams that are nearer to the bottom of the dream tunnel. Those dreams that are furthest away from the waking state, at the top of the dream tunnel, have a far greater horizon and are nearer to our worlds. That is why some claim to have been contacted by relatives during their sleep period. When they relate this to their friends, no doubt they hear the reply-" It's your imagination. That is a correct statement

I'm sure that in previous chapters we have alluded to the fact that the mind is divided into an infinite number of layers, one of which is called imagination-the ability to see, hear, touch, smell and taste without the aid of the five physical senses. It is only this layer of your mind that we may use to give you visions, thoughts and feelings, for the emotional layer of the mind is imagination's next door neighbour. Clairvoyance, clairaudience and clairsentience all make use of the imaginative layer of the mind. It is not only there for your use, but also for ours and what is more, it's scope is far wider during sleep and dream state than in waking consciousness. It makes sense to state that those who have developed the imaginative layer of the mind, make better sensitives/mediums than those who have not. The dream state affords access to all information collected in the evolvement of your mind. It is no wonder that some say, " I had a strange dream" , for it's content may be drawn from experiences far away from the present incarnation. The waking state is a barrier to great achievements, for imagination is confined mainly to experiences gained in the consciousness of the waking state.

Communication during dreaming is not limited to words, but embraces the facilities of emotion, telepathy, music as well as many other forms of art. The term communication does not only refer to information from our worlds to yours, but also from your own deeper mind, sub-conscious, unconscious and soul, through to your conscious. Remember the fact that you do not have to be asleep to dream-you do not have to be unconscious. There is such a thing as day-dreaming. We know that most good mediums receive their information in either day-dream state or unconscious trance.

The mind, and sometimes the etheric body, is more free to travel during dream state, thus giving a plausible explanation for daja-vu and precognition. Dreaming then, gives the mind an opportunity to visit or have visions of earthly places and people. It also gives an opportunity to reach the top of the dream tunnel, enter our worlds-the worlds of the mind and spirit, where you can join your departed friends and receive inspiration for future earthly experiences.

My friend, Phillipe(Armand) has already made reference to the hypnotic effect of newspapers, television, wireless and the words of other people. Is it not true that often when you watch your moving pictures, you are in a somewhat day-dream state? If this be true, you are more susceptible to their effect.

Full consciousness is a barrier to telepathy. How many of you can hold telepathic communication with your friend, whilst you are fully conscious? Is it not true that often when you are day-dreaming about your earthly friend, they telephone you or write you a letter. It is therefore much easier for your spirit friends to exchange thoughts with you whilst you are either dreaming, in sleep state or day-dreaming. I must confess that during my earthly life, many of the ideas with regards to separation of frequencies in wireless and other inventions for which I am credited, came to me during sleep, dreams or day- dreams. That is why, earlier in this chapter, I said, " Dream well".

All stimulations of the five physical senses pass through the brain to the mind-that infinite memory store of it's own evolution. Do not be surprised then if sometimes your dreams are not relative to the things that you remember. The dream world is part of the mind world-our world. Consciousness is part of the world of matter, a temporary world.

Many of you may say, " I cannot remember my dreams". Others do. Only a very few, who pass through the dream tunnel into our worlds are able to remember. Those who do remember, like those who have a near death experience, do not want to return to earthly conditions. If you only enter the more earthly bottom level of that tunnel, you may be pleased to wake up. That great intelligence, whatever God may be, in his wisdom saw that memory of dream visits to the home of the mind, would interfere with the very purpose of earthly incarnation. I once again repeat-dream well. " I'll see you in my dreams". Good-bye for now.

(Oliver and friends).

CHAPTER 12

"IF I ONLY HAD TIME"

PAST, PRESENT, FUTURE

In previous chapters we have many times referred to limitations that exist in earthly conditions. Since you live in a world of matter, you are governed by certain physical laws such as speed, distance, time, gravitation, mortality and many more. There is a physical sun, that determines night and day, apart from the orbit and declination of your planet giving seasons. Reference is sometimes made to the 'ice age', the time when dinosaurs roamed the earth, the stone age, the industrial revolution and general history-the past.

Today you have space-travel, computers, television, radio and all the marvels of modern technology-the present.

Your astronomers and weather forecasters can give a good idea of whether to expect rain, wind or sun. Doctors can give an idea of life expectancy and even the sex of the unborn baby. All of these things and more point to future events. A lot of what happens in the present is a result of what happened in the past, just as the events of the present may influence the future.

It is interesting to reflect on whether what has happened in the past, what happens today and what happens in the future is all pre-ordained.

Astronomers can give us a certain amount of information about the solar system and how planets were formed. Geologists are able to tell us about the past movements of land and seas. In the same way biologists postulate how life developed to it's present stage. It is true that we have learnt much about the planet on which you live, but allot of mysteries about it remain unsolved. Who built the megaliths? How were the pyramids built? How did life first start on earth? When did man first manifest? Was there only one big bang in creation? I'm sure that readers could add a million more questions. A lot of the past is still beyond the grasp of even the most intelligent.

If, by the present we mean your present minute, hour or day, even knowledge about that illudes you, for the breath that is taken by some at this very moment, may be their last in this incarnation. The present then, is nearly as uncertain as the past.

It is fairly accepted that day follows night, that winter follows autumn. Even the appearance of certain comets, satellites and other heavenly bodies can be predicted with reasonable accuracy. Whether you live to an

110

old age, marry a certain person, have children, become rich, poor, famous or infamous are all questions that cannot be answered-or can they? All these questions and many more about the future are the quest of most people. Unfortunately, this seems to be the main reason why people visit tarot readers, palmists and even mediums. The most important question about the future should be 'Is there life after physical death?

If there is, and intelligences dwell in those infinite levels of consciousness, one would think that they should be able to tell you about past, present and future-especially those who dwell in higher levels. Why don't they? Why don't we? If your invisible friends are able to see a little further ahead than yourself, why don't they furnish you with the name of the grand national winner or numbers that would enable you to win a lot of money?

These mysteries of past present and future were all meant to be. If all knowledge about these three eras were readily available, it would surely take away the very purpose of life, either in your earthly world or our worlds. If as we say, evolvement of mind and spirit is infinite, then so is knowledge and wisdom. Those of us who dwell in spheres capable of communicating with you, do not have the answers to all the mysteries and secrets of creation. Those who do, have left those seven spheres attached to planet earth. One of the reasons for earthly incarnation is to search for knowledge of past, present and future. If all knowledge was readily available, there would be no need for geologists, biologists, astronomists, scientists or any other " ists". Life on earth would not be a nirvana-it would be boring. It is only the struggle of life that gives it a purpose. This does not only apply to those who are incarnate but equally to those who are now discarnate. Was Newton or Einstein correct in their theories, or did both ignore the forces that prevail outside physical observations and laws?

It is true that certain people seem to have the facilities of both retrogression and premonition. These are the exceptions rather than the rule. Experiments in meditation and hypnosis suggest that it is possible for some to get a glimpse of the past. Prophets, seers and mediums can often foresee the chain of future events. They cannot demand them but receive them when they are meant to be received. From where do these visions of past and future come?

The answer is twofold. Access to the sub-conscious and unconscious of oneself gives far greater insight than that obtained through consciousness. At the same time, every person is surrounded by discarnate friends who try to guide you in your needs-not your wants. Even so, they can only share with you the knowledge and wisdom that they have gained in the evolvement of their own minds. It is limited. Just as you can often be wrong when you try to give good advice to your earthly friends, so it is that we also can make mistakes.

With regards to the future, we realise that you, like us, have free will to choose the pathway of life that you wish to tread. Your invisible friends may have a wider view and know that the pathway that you have chosen is not correct, but realise that by your mistakes you will learn. If they could truly tell you what lay ahead in the twists and turns of your life, you may not want to go round one of them, especially if there was some hard and painful lesson to be learnt. We advise you to try to listen to the inner self, as well as those few who have that special gift-" To one is given the gift of prophesy".; Not to everyone, only very few. The same applies to all other gifts.

The past. I should only speak of the past that I knew. The mental and physical mediumship of mediums whom I and my friends witnessed, proved beyond doubt that there were laws outside the realms of physics. Telekinesis showed that objects could be moved without any known force being applied to them. Tables and other objects that rose into the air displayed the fact that in certain conditions, the laws of gravity did not apply. History suggests that well before my earthly life, similar 'miracles' took place-the miracles of Jesus and other great teachers. Non of these things have given a real conviction of survival, only to the few who were able to be present at the time.

The present. Quantum physics and mechanics of the present prove that two sub-atomic particles behave in identical manner, as if they were telepathic, yet few of those involved in these experiments except the reality of animate telepathy. The same scientists, in their research even feel that there are parallel universes, but fail to look further for the intelligence's that dwell in them. Due to the emphasis on materialism, few good physical mediums are available in your present day. Although many claim to be mental mediums, most are good or bad sensitives, therefore proof of survival seems to be dwindling away. Your modern advancements in technology enable you now to photograph the aura, yet few are interested in the meaning of it's colours. The gift of prophesy also seems to have sunken to the depths of fortune telling. The tribal wars of the past seem to have increased in number, only bullets, guns, bombs and atomic weapons have replaced bows and arrows. The greed of the past seems to have flourished at the expense of communal responsibility and service to others. All ages have had, do have, and will have there philosophers and spiritual leaders. Your present is no exception, but mankind seems to prefer reading, seeing or listening about the more base passions of life than the words of a good Indian teacher. " Nobody wants to listen-and yet" -the title of the first book which we were able to transcribe through this channel. The song, " What a wonderful world" , applies only to nature and those creatures below human incarnation. In chorus and harmony we sing to you, " What a sad, sad world" and" Where have all the flowers gone". What hopes then for the future?

The future. The pendulum of God swings. As we said at the beginning of this chapter, the past effects the present, as the present affects the future. It has swung from an age of darkness, into an age of light. Generally speaking, it has also passed through the age of superstition and the age of reason into an age of materialism. The graph of that age has just reached it's maximum (Max=dy/dx). It is on it's way into a new age, when it will be realised that non of these ages has given the happiness for which mankind has been searching. In saying this, we realise that we have already stated that the future is hard to forecast because of man's free will, but a bird's eye view, or should I say, the spirit worlds view of your world can see great changes ahead. When mankind first emerged from the animal world he asked, "From whence did I come and whither do I go". Only the dawning of a new spiritual age will give a complete answer to those questions. Already those who experience astral projection and the near death experience are ready to be burnt at the stake for suggesting a differentiation between brain and mind. There will be a sweeping clean of the materialistic age as man begins to realise that his modern technology is not king. The forces of the mind are far superior to anything material. We can see that there will be a greater urge to investigate these forces. Only when this investigation is complete, will it be accepted that everything material is temporary and that the forces in the world of the mind are permanent. As the words of a song says, " Look around and you'll find me there". It is only a song's way of saying, "Seek and ye shall find" Once again we give thanks to those who have-read on.

A combined effort

CHAPTER 13

"ETERNALLY"

Ollie here. Many who read these chapters may well say-" If this medium is inspired by Oliver Lodge and friends, one would have expected information of a more scientific nature". I have previously stated the fact that the writings of Myers, myself, Richet and other friends here were written in a style not suitable for the average person. I have admitted that in my case, I used words that I knew were outside the understanding of the average educated person. In my days, the books that I and my friends wrote, were written in a sense of competition. Now we feel the importance of sharing our thoughts and experiences, with others, rather than trying to give the impression of personal greatness and education. The words that you read are a translation of thoughts transmitted. That is why you will find no references to information contained in other books.

The physical laws of conservation of matter and energy have stepped aside for more important laws, for neither of these two laws took into consideration life. The wood that was burnt, seemed less in quantity when it turned to ash, but the laws of physics proved that the chemicals involved in this process were equal. -Conservation of matter. The energy in raising a weight to a height is equal to the energy produced when that weight falls the same distance-the conservation of energy.

Both of the aforesaid laws were true in the fact that neither matter or energy ever seems to get lost, but merely transformed. Why then, cannot life be said to never really go out of existence, but merely transform from one form to another? -caterpillar to butterfly-man to spirit. The conservation of matter explains what happens to the body at physical death, but it does not make any reference to the constancy of life. In previous chapters I have made reference to the fact that there would be no awareness of electricity, magnetism or gravity if they did not affect matter. In the same way, those higher animate forces of life within the etheric world have to use matter in order that you may know of their existence. Life is drawn from an infinite number of reservoirs which contain the fluid of life in different frequencies. In some reservoirs the specific gravity of the fluid of life is so great that it's viscosity enables it to be conscious of it's own existence and individuality-like individual droplets in water vapour.

In the same way as one permanent magnet may produce an infinite number of magnetised steel needles those reservoirs of life and spirit may supply life to an infinite number of earthly bodies, whether they be virus, plant, animal or human. When life has finished with it's temporary physical manifestation it returns to one of those reservoirs-which one, depends on whether it has managed to raise it's mind specific gravity. Life is eternal-hence the choice of song at the commencement of this chapter.

To you who have managed to read on, I realise that these thoughts are just an hypothesis. The alternative is that life just emerged out of chaos, that there is no intelligence behind anything in creation, that all brain and mind are one and the same. The venus fly catching plant would disagree with this statement. The creeping vine, the same, for they seem to manage to behave intelligently without a physical brain or obvious nervous system. Ornithologists, biologists and other " ists" , recognise the behaviour patterns of swarms of insects, flocks of birds, schools of fish, yet seem content to accept that these patterns are a result of brain activity. Another song emerges from the mediums mind-or is it brain? -" When will they ever learn".

In the communications that our worlds are able to have with you, it is natural for some to expect those of us who have died to supply all answers with regards to the mysteries and secrets of creation. Not so. When we are fortunate to find a suitable channel, we can only share our thoughts with you. Even memory of earthly existence is gradually put to one side so that absolute proof of eternity is virtually impossible. If it were, there would be no need for faith and hope.

I know no more now about the origin of planets and life on them, than I did when incarnate. My feelings still tell me that the earth happened to be the right size for the holding of an atmosphere and the production of water. The chemical constituents on earth, particularly carbon and water gave the opportunity for more complex molecules to be formed-so complex that they gave life the chance to manifest. Life gradually blossoms into mind, and eventually becomes so developed, that it becomes conscious of itself, of it's own being. We have already said that in it's progression through the many forms of life, it becomes individualised. Having gained individuality, the vibrations of mind become more refined, until the term 'spirit' would be a better description. In simple language, the drivers in all our levels of mind and spirit, had to wait until the nature of earth produced many types of motor-cars-simple, belt driven at first, but later much more sophisticated, before they could give that car locomotion and intelligence. You are in a visible motor car, your earthly body, and are now on an eternal journey. We are just a little further up the same road driving an invisible etheric car. We can get out of ours a little easier than you can get out of yours..

(OLIVER)

CHAPTER 14

"TRY TO REMEMBER"

We and other groups in our level of mind, take what opportunities there are, to express our thoughts through this and other channels. In so doing we realise that those who are willing to listen, naturally wish to verify our identity, before accepting what we have to say. In previous chapters we have already stated that being re-born is very similar to earthly birth. Not many can remember the level of mind they vacated, just before birth. As time passes some do claim to have a glimpse of a previous existence-but only a glimpse.

" To thine ownself be true" ,

As you wish us to be true to you"

Forgive the biblical quotation. Is it not true that in earthly life, as you grow older, some of the chapters of youth seem like another incarnation? I want to take this opportunity to stress the fact that life in one of our levels of mind is very similar in that respect. Dying does not provide one with an infinite memory. Apart from this fact, some of us have tried to inform you that the education, intelligence, wisdom and telepathic rapport of the medium concerned, plays an equal part in deciding whether we are able to transmit a specific name of person or place.

As I continue thoughts on this matter, I 'remember' a time when my wife Mary, saw a lady by the name of Madam Vera. This was in the early 1900's. Madam Vera described a certain house, which at the time we had no knowledge of whatsoever. I think it was during the time when I was principle of Birmingham university. I'm trying to remember. When I retired from that university it was the desire of my wife and I to be in the country. We did try one or two houses but finally in a communication through Mrs Leonard, my son Raymond informed me that he had found a house for us. Through my friends Lord and Lady Glenconner, we were offered a house that they owned and it fitted the exact description given by Madam Vera all those years ago. Although we have made comments with regards to prediction, it does seem that in certain circumstances, a vision of the future is accessible, but only when friends in our dimensions give their guidance and help. Even then we have to be prepared to listen. I want to add to whatever I have said before, the fact that those of us in the mind world can influence the minds of those willing to listen, so that a reasonable idea of future events can sometimes be given and received. They cannot be demanded.

With regards to memory, I sympathise with this particular medium for there must-in fact there are times when those of little understanding demand to be given facts concerning the lives of both myself and my friends here. We cannot always remember, and even when we can, we only have the tool of telepathy to use in order to transmit the required information.

Applying thoughts of memory to the practice of hypnotic or meditative regression, not all are able to remember previous lives. Some unconsciously put together an imaginative life based on all experiences gathered since the time of individuality. In other words, it is not a specific memory of a previous life. Because of these facts the debate concerning reincarnation still remains unsolved. Once again, concerning memory, if regression is possible and the fact that we have all progressed through the many manifestations of life, how many of us remember being in the plant, animal or other worlds? It would seem true that as mind progresses, learning more and more, it throws out those memories and experiences of the past, that no longer serve any useful purpose.

We have stated that our world is in many ways similar to yours. We are all on the same journey, whether incarnate or carnate. Surely then, you can accept the fact that as we learn more and more we too put aside those memories which we feel are no longer necessary. Some things in our earthly lives we may have felt were trivial, yet you may feel they were important, and question the fact why we are not able to remember them. Other events of our lives, that you might feel were quite trivial, could well remain in our memory for quite a long time. Is it not true, that when you are able to see a GOOD medium, the facts that your friends are able to transmit through that medium seem unimportant to you. I was present, the other day when the mother of the medium's wife was able to refer to the time when she lost her false teeth on the beach. The medium's wife may well have thought that there were more important events to which the mother could have referred. These facts were given through a young lady who at the moment does not even consider herself to be a medium. One day the name " Amparo" , will be better known than it is today.

If you can accept that it is no longer necessary for you to have memory of life in the bird, fish, insect or animal world, because you have progressed to your present level of mind, then you must equally accept the fact that those who now dwell in very high levels of mind and spirit, have put away most, if not all of earthly memories. Those who dwell in those high levels of mind are more concerned with the welfare of the planet, the solar system and even of creation. Only we, and others in our levels of mind, are concerned with informing mankind, that we still live, and are not very much further along the infinite road of progress.

When we are fortunate to reach a high standard of thought transmission through this and other channels, many ask us about our previous lives. They naturally think that because we have died, 'passed over', had our 'transition', or whatever, we should have access to all previous experiences. Although we may have shed the handicap of the body, we find ourselves in a very similar situation to those of you still with a body, in the sense that memories of all that has gone before has faded. I try to explain that we in this group would rather look towards the excitement of what the future holds for us. Maybe we should contact Madam Vera.

At the very beginning of this second book, we said that we were going to introduce each chapter with an appropriate song title, and we have tried to do so. Forgive me if I bring one or two into the middle of this chapter, but I feel they might add to what we are trying to transmit. The daughter of this medium often sings a song entitled

"MEMORY"

" Memory-All alone in the moonlight.
I can smile at the old days.
Life was beautiful then.
I remember the time I knew what happiness was.
Let the memory, live again. "

Each time we are able to address groups of people, I pray that our memories are able to live again, sufficient for you to know that we are only a thought away.

Memories are not only applicable to people, but also to objects, hence the science, if that is the correct description, of psychometry. We feel that this science is the infant school of mediumship. It would appear that certain people are able to take hold of an object and give it's history. On one of my many visits to Mrs. Piper, I remember taking a watch that belonged to my uncle Robert. On this occasion, uncle Jerry seemed to communicate through Mrs. Piper, saying, " This is my watch" , and gave many details with regards to experiences he had shared with his brother Robert. Those experiences were certainly not within my memory, so the question remains-how did Mrs. Piper receive the information.

Before the death of his first wife, this medium, Raymond took a lock of his wife's hair to a medium by the name of Fanny Higginson. The medium was able to say that the hair belonged to his wife and also that his wife was terminally ill. It would seem that the hair was able to give the information as to how many children there were as well of alot of other known information. The medium also said that the wife would die as the leaves fell and the fact that Raymond would marry the lady who is now his second wife. " There will be four children altogether" , said the medium. " You don't want anymore, do you" asked the medium. She said, " There will not be any more". Without invading Raymond's privacy any more, it is sufficient to relate the fact that his present wife had to have an operation which prevented her from having children.

I relate these true stories so that readers may realise that objects not only hold a store of historic information, but also act as a stimulant for a link with our worlds. I suggest to readers who happen to meet a good medium, that they take with them a personal object that belonged or belongs to someone about whom they are concerned. Finally let us add that the intelligent mind would accept the fact that planet earth is just one of an infinite number of planets within creation, upon which life in some form manifests. Those who give thought to reincarnation, seem to only apply it to evolution on earth. Your mind and spirit has evolved through experiences, not only on earth, but in many other galaxies, where physical life manifests. The vehicles of life may differ greatly from those on earth, but the mind and soul require far more experiences than earth can provide. We have already stated that it is not easy to remember previous earthly lives. It even more difficult to remember experiences in other parts of God's universe.

OLLIE AND FRIENDS.

CHAPTER 15

"THE FINGER OF SUSPICION POINTS AT YOU"

I realise that in using the above, they may only be part of the words of a song. However, they are appropriate for the thoughts that we wish to send. Many who are still reading on, must be aware that in the past, the finger of suspicion has pointed at not only myself, but many of my friends.

It has been suggested that my friend William Crookes was having an affair with the medium, Florence Cook, and because of this he grossly exaggerated the results and capabilities of that young medium.

The close invisible friend of this medium-Franz Anton Mesmer was also accused of being a charlatan, even though many were cured as a result of his healing with magnets.

Phillippe-Armand Marie Jaque Chastenet who was really responsible for your today's hypnosis, was similarly ridiculed by the medical profession of his day. Without going through the lives of all in this group, it can be said that the finger of suspicion has pointed at each one of us. Some have suggested that the medium whom we are indeed privileged to use is a charlatan and a fraud. You who have seen us transmit our thoughts through the medium of his mind, must admit that if so, he must be one of the best. We know that he is a fellow seeker of truth, but like ourselves and all great inventors and philosophers of the past, he must prepare himself for scepticism and criticism. We would like to take the opportunity of repeating a biblical quotation, " Judge not that ye be judged". I have previously mentioned the fact that Charles Mercier wrote a book criticising the fact that I, as a scientist should not have become involved in the research involving mediums. My friend Conan Doyle also suffered during his earthly life when he suggested the existence of fairies. The finger pointed at him. With regards to the existence of fairies, and in defence of my friend Conan, there are indeed elemental spiritual beings.

This needs more clarification. Let me once again affirm that in the world of the mind, it is possible, just by thought to simulate any of earth's activities. Those readers who have read any of my books would know that my son Raymond stated in communication, that he could partake of a whisky and soda. In lower levels of mind, one can similarly take part in the simulation of the sexual act. In other levels, there are those whose desire is not just lust, but the desire to procreate. If it be the mutual desire of the two minds involved, then a mind baby can be born. In the first book, I explained that the trees, flowers and everything that exists in any level of consciousness, does so by the creative ability of the minds of the inhabitants. The life force for everything that exist in either your earthly world or our worlds, is drawn from the appropriate level of mind. If the desire be for a whisky and soda, the substance for it's mental creation is drawn from the lower forces in the etheric-those levels in which the elementary forces of law and order exist. Flowers, trees, grass are mentally constituted from their level of mind, which is obviously higher than that of whisky and soda. Those of us who wish to have animals, fish, insects or whatever, mentally create a vehicle from those levels of non individualised mind. From that level of mind that is just ready for individuality, is drawn the spirit, soul and energy necessary for that etheric baby. This being has never incarnated on earth as an individual, but as it benefits from it's parents, it may be seen on earth, as an elemental, fairy or in whatever form it wishes to be seen by those sensitive enough to become aware of it's presence.

It should be stated that there are desire levels in each of those infinite levels of consciousness. Naturally, the desires of the individuals in every level differ. Those in higher levels of mind, have had the experiences of fatherhood and motherhood many times and now desire experiences of a much more spiritual nature. I do hope that the words written are in accordance with the thoughts we are transmitting. We are trying to tell you that the conditions that prevail in all levels are in accordance with the necessary experiences and desires of the inhabitants. We do pray that our friend Raymond will not be persecuted or ridiculed for telling our truth.

Either Darwin's theory of the origin of species holds at least some truth or " God said, let there be light" , and everything else that manifests on your earth. If the latter be correct then that finger points at the astronomist's theories of how the solar system came into being and how life gradually evolved. Should the former be true then that finger points at religion in general. If we were asked which of these two was correct our reply would be, " Both" , for there must be some infinite intelligence behind the whole of creation. Should we be asked which religion is the true religion, our reply would be" All religions contain some elements of truth but none are aware of all knowledge and truth".

Not all scientists can be correct, for often the theories of one would contradict those of another. Religions point the finger at one another, for each feel they hold THE TRUTH. The same finger can often be pointed at those of us who communicate from our worlds to yours, for some contradictions are given, especially to reincarnation and the conditions that prevail after physical death.

Surely it is time for that finger to be pointed at oneself, in a realisation of one's own limitations in knowledge, experience, intelligence and wisdom with regards to THE TRUTH. This suggestion applies not only to those who still dwell upon earth but also those of us who have put the mortal coil to one side. Those religions that suggest the physical body will one day resurrect and all the atoms of the body re-assemble may have ignored the existence of the etheric body which could be said to be semi physical. It is true that one day, after passage through the dream tunnel, the etheric body will resemble the physical that it left behind. There will be a resurrection, not of the physical but of the semi-physical.

Many involved in Spiritualism deserve equal criticism for they seem to believe what they want to believe. They feel that they are going to join their loved ones for eternity, and do not realise that love extends far wider than those whom they knew in their present incarnation. Spiritualists often state that in the 'Spirit world', there is no such thing as time. That may well apply in those higher levels but does not apply in those levels still close to earth-those who are earthbound. Many feel that they have the gift of mediumship when in truth they are only a little more sensitive than their materialistic neighbour. Because of this, many gullible listeners are deceived and led on the wrong pathway. It is not surprising that those scribes who contributed to writings in the bible would say, " Thou shall not consort with mediums". Maybe in their days they did not have any Mrs. Piper's or Leonard's.

We want to destroy the myth that in heaven one walks around with wings and a white robe, playing a harp or whatever. It is our desire to put superstitious ideas in both science and religion, to one side and replace them with both truth and sense regarding those conditions in which you will find yourself after physical death. We are very fortunate to have a channel who does not inhibit the expression of truth, because of his own thoughts and ideas. Although we have stated the fact that reincarnation is a fact, we know that Raymond would like to feel that he will always be Raymond. In one sense he will, but in another, he will realise that the body of Raymond is only one mask that he holds in front of his soul. If you have continued to read, and still willing to read on-another song-" Congratulations" Good-bye for now.

OLLIE AND FRIENDS

CHAPTER 16

"HOW WONDERFUL TO KNOW"

"SOMEWHERE"

As we mentioned at the commencement of this book, we thought it befitting to commence each chapter with the title of a song. In this particular chapter we have chosen two songs. If music be the food of love-play on.

The mind of this medium is constantly seeking answers to the many mysteries of birth, life and death, hence the choice of the first song. This gives us an opportunity to answer some of Raymond's thoughts, instead of quoting some of the questions asked by those whom we address. At the same time, we readily admit that we may only share our thoughts with both him and yourselves. We do not have the answers to everything.

He, like ourselves in life, has witnessed the birth of not only his children, but many grandchildren. When one first looks at the newly born, they seem devoid of those higher parts of mind, sense of beauty, logic, intellect and many others. They like a fledgling, puppy, kitten, tadpole or any other young life seem to only have the basic instincts of self preservation. Tears only come as a result of hunger or pain, rather than the emotions of joy or sorrow. It seems marvellous how the joining of a microscopic sperm and egg can produce such a complex body, whether it be that of human or other forms of life. My friend Charles has suggested that the elemental and vital parts of mind are passed from parents to children. This is done by genes, d. n. a. molecules, etc. At the same time, I feel that the position of planets and other satellites at the time of birth, do have some effect on the personality of the baby. Some of my children physically resembled my wife, myself or grandparents, yet were very different in character and personality. It has also been mentioned that if one of my dogs ate some steak, the steak would, in the digestive process, turn into dog cells. If I ate the same piece of steak it would turn into Oliver Lodge cells. There are obviously other directives in life, besides those provided in the molecules provided at birth by our parents. Either mind, soul or spirit enters the body that forms in the mother's womb, or we are born with only that given to us by our parents and have to develop the physical brain until it can show the results of the experiences given to it by the five physical senses. If this be so, then people like Mozart must have had more than a wealth of experience in the first three years of life. You must sometimes wonder whether there is any truth in that saying, " He(or she) is a very old soul, meaning that at birth they brought a wealth of experience from the mind world into the newly formed body. " How wonderful to know" the answers to all the perplexing questions with regards to birth.

If you have read and accepted all that we have said, you will be able to accept the fact that many humans are indeed older souls than others. Without extending this chapter more than necessary, it must also be realised that this fact does not only apply to the human race, but to every other form of life. It is obvious that some of your dogs, horses, cats or other friends are more developed than others within the same species

The life that follows birth is equally mysterious. We now realise more than ever, that mind utilises and dominates matter whether it be inanimate or animate. It uses it as an instrument of learning. The physical brain does not see, hear, smell, touch or taste. It is simply a tool of the mind. A parallel could be made to a transceiver, in the fact that the brain receives impressions from the mind, as well as transmitting the impressions gained through the five physical senses. The constituents of your bodies are constructed from animal and vegetable matter, put together by that part of mind called life. In life, the dog or duck is just as capable as you, of hearing the music of Mozart, but they have not developed that higher part of mind which is capable of appreciating the harmony, beauty and emotion contained in the sound. Scientists and philosophers often make reference to beauty and complexity of physical bodies, but none are capable of understanding it's driving force-the mind. Every musical instrument requires a musician to play it. The musician needs the guidance of the composer, in the form of musical scores. Composers need the inspiration of those more accomplished than themselves. The chain is endless, and life is just one small part of it. The purpose then of life is an opportunity for learning. As we have stated in previous chapters, life's school needs many text books, hence the dualities of health and illness, beauty and ugliness, joy and sorrow, pain and ecstasy-and thousands, no, millions more. Accept life as the infant school of learning, in which you may learn the necessary basic principles, before moving on to the primary school in which the group and many of your friends now exist. If the lessons learnt in earth's infant school have not sufficiently equipped you for the etheric primary school you may have to return and return until paper and pencil are no longer necessary. In our etheric primary school, mind is quite capable of remembering that which is needed and dispensing with that which is no longer required. We still need our etheric garment, for there are as many lessons to be learnt in our world as there are in yours. Here, although the scenery may be similar, the laws of locomotion, construction and destruction are different. Occasionally, just as you take off your clothes and bathe in the light of your physical sun, we can take off our etheric garment and bathe in the light given off from those spheres and levels that are higher than the one in which we dwell.

Death-Raymond's great fear. He does not yet realise that physical death in your world is rather like etheric death in ours. In other words, death is only rebirth into a different environment. There is no death, only transition from one state to another. Many in our worlds fear birth into earthly life, just as much as Raymond fears birth into the etheric worlds. Some in your world look forward to ceasing the trials of earthly life, and entering the etheric. Not everyone fears death. We feel that religious ideas which have been placed in minds of people, have contributed greatly to the fear of death. The notion of survival, in many religions, is a resuscitation of the physical body, when the graves would open and the atoms of your body would mysteriously rush together, so that you could suffer once again. Nonsense. The atoms of your physical body have been used to create other vehicles of life, whether they be insects, worms or birds. That day of the great resurrection would virtually destroy those other forms of life, if their atoms were needed to reconstitute your physical body. The truth is that you and all living creatures are not confined to mortality. Death is a freeing from the limitations of mortality-an opportunity to enter the permanent worlds, in which there is no decay. It is time that the fear of death was replaced by a rejoicing in the fact that those who depart the earthly life, simply take off the visible clothes of the mind and replace them by less visible garments. That is the reason why I and my friends prefer to call our worlds-invisible worlds, rather than spirit world. The true spirit world lies ahead or at the top of the mind world. The celestial world lies ahead or at the top of the spirit world. Many who now dwell in those higher levels of mind, spirit and celestial levels are invisible to us, just as we are invisible to you. In the first book, our teacher suggested that you are like the caterpillars on the cabbage leaf and we are more like butterflies. Into what does the butterfly change after it's physical death? ?

At the beginning of this chapter, we quoted the title of two songs, and so far we have only concentrated on, " How wonderful to know" , hoping that we may have given one or two answers. The second song, was" Somewhere". If we may be permitted to change some of the words, we would sing-

" There's a place for you
Somewhere, a place for you,
Peace and quiet and open air
Wait for you -Somewhere
There's a time for you

Someday a time for you
Time together with time to spare
Time together with time to share
Time to learn, time to care
Someday-somewhere
You'll find a new way of living
You'll find a way of forgiving
SOMEWHERE

We pray that the writers of this song, which we have stolen from Raymond's mind, will forgive us for changing it's words. At the same time we congratulate the writer for putting into a song some of the truths which we have been trying to transmit. There is a place for you-somewhere-that depends on how much learning and progress you make in that infant earthly school. Peace and quiet-one man's meat is another's poison. As we have stated, if your desires are peace and quiet, then you will have peace, quiet and open air. They all wait for you-somewhere. There is certainly a time for you-time to spend together, time to learn, time to care and time to spare. I play golf. You will find a new way of living and one day a way of forgiving all those whom you could not forgive, when you were living on earth.

The remaining words of this wonderful song continues,

"Hold my hand and we're halfway there
Hold my hand and I'll take you there
Somehow, someday, SOMEWHERE"

Those who are willing to listen are certainly halfway , if not all the way through the dream tunnel. Your spirit friends often take your hand during dream state and take you there-to their level of consciousness and someday you too will be-" SOMEWHERE". Once again we have joined the atoms of individual minds to form a molecule in trying to share, not only thoughts with you, but truth. For now, good morning, bon jour and guten morgen. Ich muss leider gehen. I'm sorry to say we must all go now-" Somewhere".

(A molecule of mind)

CHAPTER 17

" LIGHT UP MY LIFE"

You live in a physical world of matter. Although there are many and varied elements, there are only two essential factors in your world-force with its resulting movement. Even these could be joined to be called energy. The light emitted from your sun contributes towards the development and growth of everything that exists. It lights up your life. Because of earth's axis rotation and orbit, you have night and day, as well as all the seasons. Your light has its limitations, for its passage through space takes time. It can be deflected and reflected. Even its intensity has a maximum and one day it will not even exist in its present form, but be called either a giant or a dwarf.

Many of your religions suggest that its origin was the time when God said, " Let there be light". Astronomists would have a different opinion, for they, by observation, have been able to conclude that the sun is but one of an infinite number of stars within an infinite number of galaxies. Who speaks the truth? Both. If the days of the week could be interpreted by millions of ages, then it is possible for creation to have been accomplished in six days. The biblical six days refer to the gradual evolvement of life on your planet. Since in the world of matter, light takes not only time to travel through space, it is necessary for you to consider distance and speed.

Oliver has often made reference to the dream world in which you seem to be able to communicate with others telepathically. He has not mentioned the fact that in that dream world, you can have light or darkness. The light of that dream world does not depend upon a physical star. On what then does it depend? It depends upon the spiritual level of your mind. It would also be apt to mention once again, that in that dream world distance and time do not seem to exist, except in what are termed the lower levels. Oliver has also stated that the dream world is that tunnel though which you pass on your way to our worlds. Religionists may give other terms, such as purgatory-the half way station, to heaven.

If I too were to use song titles to move from one thought to another, I would now sing to you, " Welcome to my world" , in which the intensity of light has no limitation, apart from the level in which it shines. Light in all our levels of mind and spirit, does not depend upon a physical sun, but rather upon the vibrations emitted by those who dwell there. In all religious teachings, it is said that God is the way, the truth and the light. It is also said that God is love. Another quotation that would be appropriate is, " Let your light so shine before men that they may see your good works". In various chapters, reference has been made to the aura that displays the colours of body, mind and spirit. Those who are able to become aware of auras, may feel they are using their physical eyes. Your true life is lit up by a light that does not depend on anything physical, but moreso by the frequencies of your mind and spirit. Just as a prism may display the rainbow colours of light emitted by your sun, the prism of your etheric eyes is able to see the light that exists in etheric wavelengths. In your earthly world, colours depend upon reflective wavelengths, and are generally stable. Grass is green. The colours and light of the mind and spirit varies according to development and that part of the mind which is being used at that instant. Just as the combination of earthly colours give white light, so the colours in our worlds, together give light, that is not only seen, but transmits feelings, thoughts and much more. It's intensity is infinite as one progresses from one level to another. The colours are brighter and able to communicate much more than the limitations of earthly language.

These radiations are not only emitted by those who were incarnate as human but by everything that exists. That is the reason why some of your spirit friends tell you that they are able to " Talk to the animals". Even the plants, trees, birds, insects and all other manifestations seem to be able to make one aware of their, " Feelings". As you will notice, I too am taking the opportunity to use some of your song titles or the words contained therein, for as Phillipe has said-here, even music is used as a form of communication. It would not be amiss to quote another of your songs-" I talk to the trees". If I too were permitted to change the words of that song, I would change them to, " I talk to the trees and they all listen to me". If I received an encore, I would sing, " Everything is beautiful".

My friends here have also used the term infinity, with reference to progression. It has been suggested that if you can accept the concept of infinite space, then why not infinite progression-eternity. Another song comes to mind. " Eternally". If infinity is a reality, then surely it can be applied to light. Instead of the words, " It's getting better all the time" , our composition would be, " It's getting brighter all the time". In every sphere; in every level of mind and spirit, the light with all its colours gets more majestic and brighter all the time. In this small transmission of thought, may I once again encourage you to not only show the light of your physical body, but also the light within your mind and spirit, so that others may wonder, from whence cometh that light. Some may even want to increase the light within their souls. Let the brilliance of your knowledge, experience, wisdom and spirituality shine so bright, that others who travel on the same pathway, may use your light to see the way. Finally, I too steal from the mind dictionary of our earthly friend. " Softly, as I leave you" , I share with you the quotation

I said to the man who stood at the gate of each year,
"Give me a light that I may tread safely into the unknown,"
And he replied,
"Go out into the darkness and put your hand into the hand of God
That shall be to you better than a light and safer than a known way"
God bless you all.
(A student of God)

CHAPTER 18

"TOGETHER"

We take this opportunity to emphasise once again that the reason for using this particular channel, is so that we may express ideas in a more simplistic style than we did in the books fore-written by all of us. Those who have read on, must wonder why this group is so constituted; why some who lived in the eighteenth century would combine with others who lived a century and a half later. It is natural for you to question why we are not with our wives or children. Which wife did we love the most? Did we love the children of our last incarnation more than those we fathered or mothered in other lives?. It is felt that some of these questions have been answered in either the first book or one of the chapters before this one. Some must question why I, Oliver Lodge do not continue to transmit in scientific terminology. There are a host of other questions that we feel science is incompetent to answer, because it deals only with that which may be apprehended by the five physical senses. Science is most useful when it can be positive but so often, it involves itself in abstractions, giving judgement on that which lies outside its ken. Astronomists fail to turn their telescopes inwards and use the microscope, just as microscopists fail to look at the stars.

It has already been explained that one of the reasons we join together in using Raymond, is the fact that he is more than interested in differentiating between brain and mind. He is also a mathematician, musician, radio amateur, and holds qualifications in physical education. This combination provides us with the necessary tools to transmit our thoughts. Since he is not a physicist, there are limitations in providing scientific information, and yet-many expect us to be able to convey memories and thoughts on physics, medicine and other interests of the group during their last incarnation. In this final chapter we would like to express our gratitude to both himself, his wife and all those who have been willing to listen. We would encourage those who have read on, to take greater interest in the reality of telepathy, for it's proof helps to show that mind is something very different than the brain.

Remember the white crow. A friend of mine stated quite correctly that if there was one white crow, then not all crows were black. If one clover leaf has five leaves then not all clovers have four. Just because many have allowed their spiritual gifts to become commercialised, does not mean that there are no Mrs. Pipers or Palladino's in your material world. Seek and you will find.

That infinite intelligence saw the necessity of providing physical senses in the physical world. Beyond the spectrum of those five senses lie the mental senses which mankind has hardly begun to use. Further still lie the spiritual senses that have hardly begun to vibrate.

This is demonstrated by qualified people who suggest-nay-hypnotise you into believing that patterns in cornfields and deserts are made by rabbits as they mate. It is natural that some tricksters claim that they are responsible for all those patterns. For some, they are. If their claim be true, then they must travel the world in an effort to delude others. Whirlwinds may sometimes be responsible for the laying down of corn, but we are not aware of any that write in Egyptian. The origin of magic is the imitation of the physical phenomena that has taken place ever since mankind first stepped on to planet earth. This does not negate phenomena whose origin is in the minds of those who now dwell in our worlds.

A friend of mine did extensive research into death bed visions. Even though they are still as prevalent, it is easier to say " Hallucination" , than devote time and study this phenomenon. " Imagination" , is the easiest answer to give to those who claim that they have near death experiences. " Telaesthesia" , is the answer given by those who cannot accept the concept of reincarnation. It is much easier to accept the astronomical observations that suggest there was a 'big bang', responsible for every galaxy, solar system, red giant, white dwarf, and other satellites. If that conclusion is true and infinity is a reality, then the results of that big bang will go on for ever and as we asked before-'Who lit the fuse'?

Darwin's theory helps to explain some of the mysteries of the evolvement of species, but what about the missing links? Could everything that exists on every planet have just happened by chance, or is it not possible that there is some great intelligence, an infinite mind responsible for everything that exists in both the visible and invisible? As you turn that telescope of your mind both inwards and outwards, you must want to sing the song, " What a wonderful world" , -a world full of secrets and mysteries, that no science or art will ever fully explain. Like those who experience being out of their body, we too can only say that we still exist.

Your modern computers may be programmed to seem to be more efficient in the game of chess than mankind. Surely it was mankind who developed and programmed that computer. For every effect there must be a cause. We can only reiterate that it is just as difficult for us to communicate with the world we have left, as it is for the butterfly to communicate with the caterpillar. Occasionally a butterfly lands on a leaf next to a caterpillar who was its brother, sister or close friend, finding that memories of the world that it left are stimulated. It flies off telling other butterflies of its experience, but other butterflies do not believe it. The caterpillar also relates to its friends, how it was able to communicate with a butterfly, but they reply, " Impossible". As your technology increases, you may explore the far regions of the universe. You may be able to make your computers labour for you, but non of these things will ever help you to understand that the greatest of all is-love.

As this chapter nears its conclusion, remember that the thoughts transmitted were from a molecule of mind, rather than from just one atom. Together we pray that you will all gather knowledge, wisdom and spirituality from the harvest of life so that you may bring it with you to share with those in your level of like mind. Together we join in harmony to change the words in a song. It's new title is, " We'll see you in your dreams. Our gratitude goes to those who have read on and particularly to this channel and his wife, who have given so much of their time and devotion in receiving our thoughts.

OLIVER

Raymond Lodge

CHAPTER. 19.

"MEMORIES"

Although they have referred in previous chapters to that part of the mind that stores memory, I feel that you should ask yourselves whether you are able to remember every chapter of your present life. To some of you, the chapters of youth must seem like a reincarnation from the chapters of infancy. In the same way, later chapters of your life seem to be the result of all previous ones. You surely feel like a different person to that when you were a young girl or boy. As father has said before, birth seems to rob you of all memories of previous existence. Some claim to be able to remember previous lives whilst others feel that life only began at birth into the present life. In previous writings, my father has stated that the mind has evolved from a state of statisticity, through all manifestations of life until human incarnations. Some of his friends have explained that death is like re-birth, yet many of you expect us to be able to remember every detail of the last physical life. Only some of you are able gradually, through hypnosis or meditation, to be able to bring back a glimpse of other experiences in the mind's journey. In living life, those who are able to get that glimpse, can use the medium of language to share their memory with others. From our levels, we are only able to use the medium of telepathy, hoping that the receiver is able to translate our thoughts into words. We need a transmitting medium, in the same way as you need a receiving medium. Mediumship is not limited to the earthly world.

The medium that I now use, once had a motor cycle accident. His only memory of that incident is that of waking up in hospital. He cannot remember the actual accident. There was no damage to his physical brain and therefore no obvious reason why memory of this accident should be obliterated. Just as the body has a defence mechanism in the form of the immune system, the mind also has several defence systems. If one could have very clear remembrance of all the traumas in physical life, it would surely fill the mind with so much fear that one would eventually be afraid of doing anything.

Similarly, if one could have clear remembrance of 'the spirit world' at birth, I am sure that there would be a desire for immediate return. Raymond also once fell whilst cleaning his swimming pool and for a short while could not recognise his wife and family. At the same time, he was able to say, " I am". Some of you may know that I was killed on September the fourteenth in the year nineteen fifteen. I still cannot remember clearly all the events that took place on that day in France. The same defence system of the mind operates in the mind world, just as it does in your world. Who wants to remember the sad events of physical life? I have tried to transmit my thoughts through a physical medium but found the barrier of negativity too obstructive to prove my identity. Without invading the privacy of that medium, it is our wish that the persecution she has suffered will not deter her from resuming her work. Maybe I should have used the song title "Laura". That is not the name of the medium, but I am sure that those who attended that physical circle will recognise the name. I take this opportunity to join my father and his friends, to verify that most of what my namesake has received telepathically is true. I have joined my father's team before, in order to add my thoughts in the form of a poem. I take this opportunity to express my thoughts in regards to memory in similar fashion, and send my love to those who received my thoughts in that physical phenomenon to which I referred. To that circle I express my apologies for not succeeding as I would have liked.

> Can the dolphin remember being a bird?
> To some, this thought would seem absurd.
> Can the lion remember being a rose?
> These questions to you I now pose
> It is true that as more you progress,
> Past memory seems to get less and less
> Events of our lives you would often ask
> To remember all is near an impossible task
> As we move from sphere to sphere
> We find it harder to you draw near
> Earthly life is just like a dream
> Yet thoughts of it you ask us to beam
> For just a moment just rest and pause
> And realise everything has purpose and cause
> Only a part of this are you able to see
> You cannot see, Franz, father and me
> Yet we are here right by your side
> To help and try your life to guide
> Onward and onward for ever we move
> This for us is so hard to prove
> Try in your lives to be loving and kind
> Then one day, in our world, you really will find
> That clearly you'll be able to see
> Your friends and relations and even-me
> (Raymond Lodge)-Thank you for reading on.

CHAPTER 20

"FEELINGS"

Allow me once again to represent all of the friends gathered around me Although we have stated the fact that we are all individual, individuality in our section of the mind world is not as important as it is when incarnate. Imagine that we are atoms of mind combined together to form one molecule. In that imagination, try to see that in each level of consciousness there are virtually infinite molecules of mind, which together constitute the whole. Remember also that great teachers of the past and present have voluntary reincarnated so that they may try to influence the minds of those who dwell on earth. In similar manner some in higher mind levels may come to lower levels in that same mind world to teach, encourage and help those who desire to progress.

You may wonder why it is that some of my friends here were born in the eighteenth century, others including myself in the nineteenth, yet we combine together in our work with you. May I once again remind you that in this consideration, you are only taking into account our last life. It is the total evolvement of mind that determines the level in which you find yourself after re-birth. In other words, although Franz and Armand came home before Charles and myself, this does not indicate that they are at this moment in higher levels of mind and spiritual development.

The great light, known to you as Mentor dwells in a much higher level than ourselves but takes it upon himself/herself/itself to help those in our molecule of mind. In Spiritualist terms you could say that he/she/it is our guide, teacher, guardian or whatever name pleases your mind. When we either individually or as a group, travel to lower levels, those who dwell there no doubt dub us as guides or teachers. Some of you who still dwell upon earth may belong to a much higher level of mind than those in this group. You may have reached individuality sooner and lived many more human incarnations than any in this group to which I belong. Whenever we have the privilege of addressing groups of people through this medium, many feel that because we have died we are more knowledgeable, wise, or spiritual than those who are willing to listen to us. This is not so. As we often say, by trying to be of service to others we also help ourselves. Many times we learn from the thoughts that you pass to us through this medium. Although I was a scientist I have a lot to learn about the arts. Charles, although professor of physiology and president of the institute of meta-physics admits that he too has much to learn. Just for your interest, in earthly life he was ten months older than myself but not ten months more spiritually advanced. Forgive my sense of humour. I mention these facts so that whenever we or others in the mind world hold communion with you, it should be realised that the only advantage we have over yourselves is the fact that we no longer are restricted by the physical. We are not necessarily wiser or more spiritual.

We take the opportunity once again to refer to the new born whose physical organs do not permit them to express their knowledge, wisdom or spiritual awareness. until they become mature. The converse also applies. The fact that some person has reached maturity does not give any guarantee of knowledge or wisdom. Mozart, a friend of Franz, was able to show his great knowledge of music at a very early age. This "fact", not opinion, serves to illustrate the possibility that your young children or friends may be more wise and spiritually evolved than yourselves.

In these final comments, let me once again add one or two more comments with regards to communication. Naturally when we have the privilege of passing our thoughts through Raymond, groups of people feel that we should be able to give any information relative to our last incarnation or even previous incarnations. We are aware that with your modern technology it is possible to access the family tree of most who have lived in England during the last two centuries. It is therefore possible that this medium has accessed my family tree and memorised most members of my family. Simply giving names or even the names of my dogs and peacocks would not be classed as evidence of my survival.

We feel that only those close friends who know him very well, would know that what he is able to give when in trance state far exceeds his normal capability. It is our prayer that when he reads these words he will take no offence. There are divers gifts. Without doubt there have always been mediums who are able to give evidence of the continued survival of family and friends. Those mediums do not necessarily have the gift of knowledge and wisdom. The group that assemble around this fellow do so in an effort to give knowledge as to the conditions that prevail in our infinite levels of consciousness.

Now that a medium friend of Raymond has come home, we feel that he would have no objection to us relating a conversation which took place when that particular medium came abroad to demonstrate his gift-'the discernment of spirit'. The name of the visiting medium was "Albert the Best". In a conversation one evening Albert said to this medium. "There is only one thing that worries me. As you know, my wife and children were killed during the last war. What if they have reincarnated when it's my turn to go". He obviously did not know that the love bond that his family had for him, and he for them, would ensure that they would be there to meet him when it was his time to shed his earthly garment. The friends who helped him in his mediumistic work did not have the gift of knowledge and wisdom even though they were able to help him give evidence to others of the survival of their friends. We can feel his thoughts at this moment wanting those who knew him to know that it really was his wife and children who were waiting when he temporally came out of his comatic state just prior to his death. I ought also to mention the fact that during a private sitting, the medium Albert, was able to give to the wife of Raymond, evidence of the fact that the Marquis de puysegur and an Austrian doctor were present. In fact, Albert asked this medium who were the friends that gathered around her. Since Raymond had not divulged the fact that we work through him, he simply said, "Oh!, my wife sits in a circle and they would be some of the people that manifest in that group". Albert now knows the truth and is still with his wife and family. We have this knowledge from sister Mary who often joins us.

There are mediums amongst you who have the gift of prophesy yet are unable to give evidence of survival. Similarly, not every medium capable of giving evidence has the gift of healing. —"There are divers gifts-To one is given the gift of ? "As a group , we would suggest that each one of you find the spiritual gift that you have and develop it to the full. Remember that in all things-it is not what you want but rather what you need and have been given. The mediums that Charles and I were able to investigate were quite happy to develop their gift to as high a degree as possible without wanting to display every gift in the list. Whoever is your finest concert pianist at the moment is not necessarily your finest violinist.

If reincarnation be a reality-and it is-then you have all come back for a purpose; to learn whatever lessons you were not able to learn in your previous evolvement of mind. You may prefer us to say-previous lives. The group assembled here all came back for a purpose. A Marquis returned to show that not all royalty bowed to the wishes of the court but instead took an interest in mind and it's survival.. An Austrian doctor took an interest in energies outside the realms of medicine. Two professors , sometimes to the disgust of their profession, devoted much of their lives to what is termed psychic research. A plumber realised that by returning to help others not to make the same mistake as he made, he would be helping to remove the doubt that lay in the mind of his son. Our teacher also expresses his thoughts through this channel, and in so doing, helps to demonstrate that there really are infinite levels of consciousness. It is obvious to all those who are willing to listen and read on, that he dwells in a level higher than the remainder of the group here. He is our GUIDE, just as we try to be yours. You do not have to wait until you come home to act as a spirit friend. Be a friend and guide to all your friends in earthly life, for there are many around you who

138

cry for knowledge and help. Do you hear them? Do you hear us? That is why we chose such titles of the two books that we have tried to transcribe through this fellow. There are not many who are really willing to listen to either yourselves or ourselves.

Take a little time away from earthly duties and work. Look around at the wonders of creation, at infinite space with all it's galaxies, planets and other heavenly bodies. Even on that spec of dust earth, the manifestations of life are sufficient for the intelligent to realise that some infinite intelligence must be the cause for this effect.

In earlier chapters we have referred to the venus fly catching plant and the creeping vine that seem to display some intelligence without having a brain in the same way as you have. We have also referred to those who claim to have had a glimpse of our dimentions during that which is now called the near death experience. Your modern means of communication inform you of many phenomena that occurs in your world. Do you question it's origin , or better still, do you go to see it?

Some of us have referred to the superstitions that still prevail in religion, yet most of you , instead of thinking for yourselves follow in the footsteps of your parents. Friends here have suggested that you allow yourselves to be influenced too much by the opinions of others, whether religion, politics or whatever.

We also take the opportunity to mention the fact that my friend Findley tries to work through another channel. At the last public meeting it was my pleasure to inform that inspired channel that it was our group who inspired Raymond and his society to finance that friend's first publications. I want to take this opportunity to thank a friend of that friend who is trying scientifically to demonstrate the reality of the etheric world.. To him, I would suggest that only when physics and mediumship work together will the fact that intelligences do exist in those parallel universes, made up of ether in ever increasing states of vibration. My son Raymond joins me once again with one of his conundrums.

> Let you and I join together in play
> As we change two letters in the name of Ray,
> To try to find the name of that friend,
> I'm sure you'll get it before we end.
> He is also a man of science.
> In that my father and he have alliance.
> The other friend same name as a saint.
> It's quite normal, it isn't quaint.
> Both friends in corn circles once went

To try find out how they were sent.
I feel that great courage they both hath.
One lives quite close to the city of Bath.
They both to many have publicly spoken,
And in so doing many fears have broken
Not only to old but also to youth
They have both tried to tell the truth
I do hope that you are already succeeding
Or shall I with clues you continue feeding?
In same paper they both often write
To tell the same truth with all their might
If you've not guessed them , I won't carry on,
One's name is Michael, the other's is Ron

To both of those gentlemen I give our gratitude for trying to replace faith by knowledge. It is only with the courage of such people that the media have been encouraged to become involved more with those unexplained energies that lie outside the realms of physics. In previous paragraphs, we have stated that the lower parts of the etheric world contain the vibrations associated with electricity, magnetism, gravitation, cohesion—the non-living etheric. A little higher in that same etheric world are the vibrations associated with life in it's initial manifestations, such as life in the virus, the single cell of your body and the amoeba. The controlling mind of such manifestations does not need male or female. They can multiply by division. As we move up in etheric frequencies, it can be seen that fertilisation is necessary in some of the plant and vegetable world. —still part of the etheric world. In the fish, bird, reptile and animal kingdoms, male and female can be seen to contribute in developing those levels of mind called emotion, intelligence and intuition. Mankind, being the upper section of the animal world, has developed those levels of mind to a sufficient degree, to enable him to retain individuality, yet he is still in the etheric world. After many attempts to raise the higher levels of mind, he can escape from the limitations of the etheric, shed his etheric garment and enter the mind world, becoming just light but still retaining individuality. After learning all the lessons of that mind world, he moves on to the world of the spirit, only when his light has increased it's intensity to jusify his progress. Eventually progress enables him to enter the celestial vibrations of the seventh sphere where he would prepare for moving away from this solar system and even this galaxy, into other regions of creation, just as the caterpillar moves on to being a butterfly. Spiritualists often refer to the earthly and spirit world as if there were only those two states of existence. In this final chapter we are trying to have you realise that there are states of mind higher than etheric vibrations; that there is the world of the mind, the world of the spirit, the celestial world, then rebirth into other parts of creation. These facts we have learnt from those who dwell in higher levels of mind than ourselves.

I'm sure that I have previously referred to the envelope that Myers left with me hoping that some medium would be able to reveal it's contents. I too left seven envelopes, one inside the other, with the same intention in mind. Both of these experiments failed, proving that communication from these infinite levels of mind is a near impossibility. Why then should those who have read on, accept that the thoughts expressed in both books come from myself and the friends who join me?

I have also suggested that no two snowflakes have exactly the same crystalline patterns. We have in your meetings encouraged you to try to transmit a thought to the person sitting next to you. All of these things help to emphasise the fact, that for evidence of continued mind survival, it is necessary to have one incarnate and one discarnate person whose minds resonate on exactly the same frequency. It is a wonder then, that any good communication is ever received from our worlds to those of you still incarnate on any planet.

Another of my friends—Arthur Findlay, in his earthly writings tried to emphasise the fact that information given to you by mediums is no proof of survival, if you already have knowledge of that information. I did not have to wait for death, to know the reality of telepathy, for I feel that it was adequately demonstrated during my earthly life —by such friends as Myers as well as others. "For those who are willing to listen—read on", and realise that only when you receive information of which you are not aware, can you question it's origin.

We have also stated, that in our opinion, there were never meant to be great numbers of wonderful mediums all incarnate at any one time. If there were, then such statements as "Seek and ye shall find", "Have faith", "Knock and it shall be opened", would be meaningless. We in this group can understand now, why mankind was meant to wonder and try to understand birth, life and death.

I do assure you that your friends and relations do, many times try to have you know that they still live, but often find the frustration of finding a suitable channel too much, and 'give up the ghost'. They soon realise the fact that since time here has a different measurement, you will soon be with them once again. With reference to what I have tried to transmit, how many of you attend spiritualist meetings, week after week, year after year, hoping that you will receive confirmation of the survival of the friends that have come home before you? Were you aware of the information that you sometimes, not often, received? Did you accept it as proof of survival? In some of your meetings, we have tried to suggest to you that much of that which you receive from sensitives and mediums may have been obtained psychometrically. Not many are really willing to listen to the truth, for often it hurts.

There is life after physical death, and your physical world is full of mysteries which in themselves suggest "That there is more to heaven and earth than mankind realises". Just because some mediums use their undeveloped gift for profit, does not mean that there are no Mrs. Pipers in your world. "Be not as the hypocrites are for they love to pray and shout in front of all". Some of the most gifted mediums do not seek publicity. "Seek and ye shall find"

Just because there are those who imitate patterns in cornfields and deserts does imply that all patterns are fraudulent. Because much of the phenomena involved in spiritualism may be imitated by magicians does not mean that all physical phenomena has an earthly origin. If one priest commits a sin, it does not suggest that all priests are sinful. The fact that no medium has satisfactorily proved survival to you does not negate the possibility of survival. The numbers of those who are just sensitive far exceed those who have true mediumistic gifts. Sensitives have their uses, and often sensitivity is the birthplace of mediumship.

Myers and I may have failed to prove survival to mankind——not surprisingly, for those who turned water into wine did not convince the whole of mankind of the reality of "many mansions". Much of that which is termed physical mediumship has been fraudulent. This does not mean that there are no true physical mediums capable of producing such phenomena as direct voice, materialisation , psychic photography, voices on magnetic tape or whatever.

My family and I obtained much evidence in using a table that responded to the thoughts transmitted by my son Raymond, as well as other communicators. Do not feel that you can only receive communication from those who people are mediums. Our small table often acted as a medium. The air is a medium used for the transmission of sound. It is not animate.

Are you content just to read books written by my friend Barrett or others about death bed visions, or do you have the courage to go and witness them yourself. It is easier to suggest that there is some biological brain process that is responsible for this, than to accept the possibility that friends who dwell in the mind worlds are there to meet you when you make that inevitable journey. It is much easier to label the stories of near death experiences as wild imagination, than to research and interview those who claim to have had such experiences. Just because you may never have seen a 'GHOST', does not mean that they do not exist. In making reference to ghosts, you will remember that we have taken pains to differentiate between a ghost and a true apparition-one being an imprint on the sensitive ether and the other a living vibration of a friend within the same ether.

"Too marvellous for words", are part of a song that I steal from the mind of this medium, and we feel that those words are very appropriate for all manifestations of matter on earth, whether inanimate or animate. As a scientist I could find no other cause for the cosmos than a big bang. A big bang at the centre of what? Creation is infinite and it is difficult to envisage a big bang at the centre of infinity. Look also in to the night sky, into infinite space and realise that the words of the above song are equally appropriate. Neither science nor religion are able to explain all the wonders and secrets in creation. Those of us who are able to express our thoughts through some medium, whether it be a table or person can only tell you that we still live— in a non material world—the mind world. Those who now dwell in what we have defined as the spirit and celestial worlds are beyond communicating with those who dwell in the lower levels of mind, etheric and astral We do not have many more answers to these mysteries than we did when incarnate. Most of your friends who come 'home', realise the hopelessness of finding some way of letting you know of their continued existence. Some still linger in the dream tunnel, not realising that they have arrived.

All of those who constitute this group—this molecule of mind —- were keen to prove survival. That is why we work together in this way, trying to accomplish the same aim. Other groups try to put their voices on your magnetic tapes in the form of what is now termed, electronic voice phenomenon. Some mischievous minds, find joy in letting you know of their survival by moving objects in your homes, not realising that by so doing, they often create fear instead of joy. Just as some galaxies are out of range of astronomist's instruments, higher levels of mind are out of range of communicating with either ourselves or yourselves.

I realise that when we successfully transmit our thoughts through this channel, some of you would say that we talked, 'above your heads', whilst others would say that Oliver Lodge and his friends should have transmitted in a more scientific manner. In the first book, we stated the fact that we were pleased to have the opportunity of expressing our thoughts in simplistic style so that more would be able to understand the complexity of birth, life and rebirth. Physical life does seem like that poor player who struts and frets his hour upon the stage and is heard no more, but we continue to assure you that off stage, there is another, nay, an infinite number of opportunities , of taking part in a different play; one that does not necessitate the changing of scenery or the dropping of the final curtain. The scenery changes automatically as you progress from one level to another and because progress is infinite, there is no final curtain.

I mentioned in the first book that in my earthly life, I used to go around with five ladies to heal those who were sick. I do pray that my friends here have helped you to understand that the greatest hindrance to all forms of healing is doubt; doubt in the mind of the healer and doubt in the mind of those who require healing. I agree with the statements made by my friends, that the greatest healing power of all is that which lies within your own mind. At the same time, it is true that, providing there is no doubt in the mind of patients, energy can flow from the auric fields of the healer to those of the patient. —Animal magnetism. We have tried to inform you that light—the light of mind and spirit exists in all levels of consciousness, and that those who were doctors or nurses in earthly life often try to transmit telepathically the energy of that light to those of you engaged in healing.

I have drawn a parallel between earthly life and a play. As well as those actors who appear on the stage there are also those backstage and do not receive the same acclaim. In spiritualism it would also seem that the clairvoyants and clairaudients receive greater acclamation than those who have other gifts. Let me try once again to emphasise that it is surely far better for some person to be healed than for them to receive information about which they are already aware, from some medium. In truth, there are divers gifts and they are all as important as one another. Applaud those who work spiritually off stage just as much as those actors whom you see on the mediums stage of life.

Some who read the first book, told this fellow that they had to read it several times. If that be the case, then my prayers have been answered, for it was my desire that my thoughts were expressed without too much digression or padding. We all pray that the same has occurred in this second book, and that it's reception will be sufficient to inspire the mind of Raymond to continue in his co-operation with us. We did warn him that sometimes, he, like ourselves, would be persecuted by those who set themselves up as authorities in communication. This statement gives us the opportunity of expressing gratitude to his wife, for without her encouragement he would have thrown in the towel many times.

Either there is life after death or there is not. If there is not, then there does not seem to be much purpose in continuing with the struggles of earthly life. If there is life after death, then it would seem common sense to discover the conditions that prevail in that after life. One could put forward the premise that all learning and progression is for the benefit of the children that follow you, for certainly technology has made great strides and mankind is materially better off than ever before. From our observations, even with greater wealth, technology, space travel, mankind is no wiser as to the origin of all things, and still seems to be involved in greed, jealousy, aggression, hatred and selfishness as ever before. Is the measure of happiness one of material things or rather one of collecting the treasures of knowledge, wisdom and spirituality? We are trying to turn your eyes from the mud of materialism to the stars of creation; to realising the truth that earth is but one of an infinite number of schools in the university of creation. If everything that exists on earth, in life and in the heavens all came about by chance, then it could similarly all come to an end by chance and there would be nothing. What is nothing? Searching again for appropriate words from some song, I find, —"Nothing comes from nothing". The fact that creation exists, tells us that it must have come from something or else always existed, but constantly changes it's form, just as you change your earthly bodies. If, as some suggest, everything happened by a process of natural selection, then there must have been some intelligence behind that selection. In these thoughts we are only appealing to that level of mind called reasoning to have you realise the fact that there must be some infinite intelligence responsible for the existence of the worlds of elemental, vital, astral, etheric, mind, spirit and celestial.

In your earthly world you have individuals that form into groups. Those groups constitute a village, town or city. Many of these form one county , province or state. Countries consist of several counties, provinces or states. Your planet has many countries of various levels of development, some being labelled third world or under developed. Some in your earthly group may have to leave for another town, city or even another country, in order to progress in their earthly life.

A parallel may be drawn here, for we as individuals form in to groups to constitute one level of consciousness. Many levels of consciousness join together to form a sphere. The seven spheres all joined together constitute what Raymond terms, 'The invisible world', for in ordinary consciousness he cannot see that world. Sometimes in our worlds one has to leave the group so that they may progress in the mind world. Just as on earth, those who have left you may sometimes visit you, so it is here in our worlds. Those who have gone a little further along the spiritual pathway can come back to see us whenever their mind feels the need of our presence. Telephones are not necessary in the level in which we dwell.

We too have under developed souls, and it is our duty to try to raise their mind level so that they may progress into higher levels. Do you help those less fortunate or developed than yourselves to climb to your level or do you ignore them and only see to your own comfort and wants? ?

Remember that in this chapter, individual minds join together to transmit thoughts. Only some of those thoughts come from the mind of

Oliver Lodge. Some come from a mind that dwells in a higher level, yet finds pleasure in helping our group. Oliver acts as chairman only because there are some still on earth who knew him before he was reborn.

The life and work of Franz, lives on, for even in your present day the word "mesmerised" is common. Had he not used his magnets and mesmeric passes, Armand(Phillippe) could never have followed in his footsteps. In so doing Armand discovered the power of suggestion and was without doubt the forerunner of today's hypnosis. He also discovered that in that altered state of consciousness, people sometimes claimed to see another world and be influenced discarnate friends. Without these two friends, my friend Myers might never have been inspired to write extensively on hypnosis in his book-"The survival of human personality". Most readers would know that Myers and I were very close friends in earthly life. He was in those days, so sure of survival that he would often say, "I'm counting the days until the holidays". He, in those words, must have felt that earthly life was either like work or prison. Bearing in mind the conditions that prevail in our level of mind—he was correct.

Charles Richet , who at this moment is stood by my side, conducted many experiments in cryptaesthesia in an effort to find from where the information came that mediums gave. In his earthly life he became convinced of the reality of materialisation, yet at the same time thought it to be absurd, and felt greater conviction of survival could be obtained through mental mediumship than physical. He still feels the same and I tend to agree with him, for often the energy involved in physical mediumship does not permit the materialised figure to give sufficient personal details to establish their survival. In his earthly life, Charles was very similar to this medium, Raymond, in the fact that he always looked for alternative explanations to explain the phenomena that he witnessed. At this moment he is saying, "Tell them that doubt was also my driving force". I have referred to one of the books that my friend Myers wrote. Let me take this opportunity to recommend that those of you who have READ-ON , should read one of Charles' books—"Thirty years of psychical research", for it contains a summary of his lifetimes work in studying all the phenomena contained both within and outside spiritualism. It was Charles who in earthly life said that the more he studied this phenomena and life itself, the more he realised the fact that he knew nothing about the universe. I concur, and having entered this level of consciousness would replace the word universe by creation, for universe generally refers to the world of matter, with all it's solar systems, galaxies and other heavenly mysteries. - This medium's father now joins us to add his final comments

Ello again-it's me, Raymond's dad. I only wanted to come in to tell ye that a feel more alive now than ever a did when a was where you are. Don't be afraid of dying-it's just like going to sleep an wakin up in another place-a bit like dreaming only it's real. Everythin that these fellers are tellin ye is true, but I never believed it when I was livin. It's dammed ard to try to find some way of gettin back to tell ye that we're still ere and livin. I tried many times to get through some o them mediums our Raymond went to see but a couldn't manage it. They couldn't ear me so a give up in th'end. That lady a told ye about made me realise that our May and Raymond would soon be 'ere and what's more a can keep me eye on 'im any time a feel he's a bit down. I don't stay around 'im all t' time because there's alot to do 'ere. It's much better than where you are. What else can a tell yer. 'av told ye every-thin a do. Don't forget to tell them 'oos a bit down, that it's no good doin anthin like I did. Ye only 'av to make up for it in some way. Anyway a 'ope our Raymond keeps goin to places then a can talk to ye. Eh!, it's grand bein able to get our Raymond to lisen to me. He never did when a was there. Tell 'im that am with 'im and I'll always be there when 'e wants me.. 'ope to see some of ye when ye come 'ere. It's true ye know—It's like bein born again only it's a better place. Anyway, ta-ra!

I sincerely hope that the father's remarks do not discourage you from staying the course of life and reaping the benefits of all earth's experiences. His remarks with regards to trying to contact those he left behind, give me another opportunity to stress the difficulties of communication.

Let me once again steal from the treasure chest of this mediums memory, and in so doing suggest to you that those who read these words, may have known some of the mediums who have quite recently joined our dimensions. Let me refer to one or two. Gordon Higginson, Albert Best and Doris Stokes number amongst those whom this fellow invited to Spain and Gibraltar to demonstrate their gifts. If such people as these could easily return and give a wealth of evidence of their survival to both yourselves and Raymond, surely they would do so, for this was their life's dream. Some who read these words may claim that such friends have achieved this. I have already admitted that Myers and I failed in this task even though we tried hard. The mediums to whom I refer may from time to time manage to succeed in transmitting the odd thought to some receiver, but to give irrefutable evidence of their continued survival is, as I said, near impossible because of the restrictions imposed by telepathy.

As you read this book you would naturally say, "How is it then that you and your group are able to have Raymond write your thoughts, when you have stated that proof of survival is nearly impossible. I remind you of the fact that if there be one white crow, then not all crows are black. Although there are not too many Mrs. Pipers in the world at any one time, there are one or two white crow mediums, but-my favourite word, - but you have to look very hard to find one. As I have previously stated, we are very fortunate in the fact that Franz's and Raymond's etheric brains resonate on nearly the same frequency, enabling us to have our thoughts transposed into nearly the right words.

Before bringing this chapter to a close, let me once again encourage those "who have been willing to read on", to not only study the work of clairvoyants and clairaudients, but also to extend their research into death bed visions, healing, near death experiences, automatic writing, psychic photography, physical phenomena, , electronic voice phenomenon, faces that appear in the floor, patterns in fields and deserts, objects in the sky, interference on your computers and a host of other phenomena that have no physical or earthly explanation. The list for suggesting the reality of the survival of human personality is far longer than any list that negates it.

Most of you who visit sensitives and mediums do so in the hope of finding out what lies ahead in your earthly lives. We, who now live in the mind worlds may sometimes have a wider view of the future than yourselves, but we cannot forecast the alterations that you may make by the exercise of your free will. The gift of prophesy is a true gift, but it is not given to every clairvoyant or clairaudient. It is a gift by itself. Do not feel that you have to rely on the spiritual gifts of others. Close your physical eyes, open your etheric and you will be surprised to find that you too have one of those "divers gifts". It may not be amongst the above list , but remember the fact that the music of great composers inspired the minds of many to realise that there is more to earth and heaven than meets the eye. This could also be said about the works of great artists and others who have found their gift. Find your gift and in so doing , let your light shine before others that they may realise that there truly is a differentiation between brain and mind. The brain many die but the mind continues on a never ending, exiting, pathway of progress and learning. In the remainder of your earthly lives, turn work into play, and the process of learning into joy. Put aside the superstitions of religion and the narrow views of science , and as you do these things, a new world will become more etherically visible—our worlds. From all gathered by my side, we wish that you use the power of your minds to gain bodily health, mental wisdom and spiritual progress.

I hope you have been intrigued by the use of song titles and words to introduce the various chapters. It would seem most appropriate to repeat those that we have already used. "We'll meet again, don't know where, don't know when, but I know we'll meet again some beautiful bright day. My gratitude to those of you who have been willing to listen and——read on.

Oliver and friends.

148

June Smith

POSTSCRIPT

"AT THE END OF THE DAY, JUST KNEEL AND SAY THANKS OH LORD FOR MY WORK AND PLAY".

At the end of the first book it was my pleasure to add a few words to those which Ray wrote in the preface. I now take the same opportunity at this, the end of the second book. Here in our Villa/Centre many people come to visit us. Some come to see if Ray can help them overcome depression, fears and phobias, whilst others come to see me for healing. Often we work together. I spend fifteen minutes giving some form of healing then my husband takes the same patient into a state of relaxation, placing positive thoughts in their mind. Oliver and his friends often remind me that body, mind and spirit are closely connected and that often it is necessary to work on all three in order to help those who need healing. Groups of people come to listen to our invisible friends talking through Ray, and recently we have been invited many times to appear on both radio and television. I must confess that on these occasions I am much more nervous than Ray, for I realise that his experience in school teaching has given him greater confidence. However, practice makes perfect, so they say. Oliver helps, by reminding me that sometimes my simple way of expression has greater effect than Ray's more complicated scientific explanations. I cannot describe the joy and comfort that I get from talking to the invisible group. They are now just as dear to me as my own earthly family.

Let me tell you of the experiences that I have when I am in bed—well, some of them!

If Ray does not slip into trance when we go to bed, he does on the following morning. I can tell who is going to speak before any words come out of Ray's mouth. Not only does his facial expression change, but he seems to take on the mannerisms of whoever is going to use him. Phillipe always smiles so much that I can even see Ray's teeth—a very rare occurrence in his normal life. Phillipe must still wear similar clothes to those which he wore when living in France, for he will often seem to adjust invisible frills on Ray's cuffs. He also uses his hands to express himself, whereas Ray is more like a statue in Madam Tusards waxworks.

I know that Ray spoke about my healing in his preface and I have little to add, although I would like to share one or two experiences with you. A Spanish neighbour of ours became a very good friend when we first moved into this villa. Since our knowledge of the Spanish language is limited, she and her husband have helped us many times. Charri had polio when she was very young and later suffered with breast cancer. Not long after we moved here, she asked if I would give her healing since secondary cancer had appeared in her other breast. I have been giving healing to Charri for the past nearly three years, but as Ray said-not everybody is meant to recover physically. My friend died only three days ago and yesterday we attended a Roman Catholic Spanish funeral service. Although my thoughts about religion may be different, I have to admit that I thought the service was excellent. The usual prayers were said and during part of the service the priest suggested that all the congregation should shake hands and kiss one another-the Spanish way, on the cheek. I thought this was lovely. One could feel the vibrations of love and sympathy passing from one to another. This is the first time I could honestly say that I enjoyed a funeral.

During the times of healing, Charri and I often spoke about invisible friends and both she and her husband have heard Oliver speak through my Ray. This gave her so much confidence in the reality of the invisible world, that when she was taken to Cadiz hospital, as she left, she looked into my eyes and said, "Good-bye June". At the funeral one of her students told me that Charri had also told her that she would not see her again. Charri knew where she was going and was ready for that journey.

Holly, another lady with a similar problem came for healing for about three months. She had an advanced cancer of the breast. Similarly, during her healing sessions we talked many times of the invisible world and of the knowledge that Oliver and his friends give us. Holly's last visit here was on a Tuesday for she had to go to a London hospital on the following day. During the healing session my husband joined me helping Holly to relax and relate that which she saw in her mind. She said that she could see many dogs of different breeds and sizes. There were also two brown and white horses. These were on the right as she looked at the sea and sky. On the left, there was an Irish lady surrounded by many children of different ages. They were all smiling at her. On the Thursday, her husband telephoned me from London to tell me that Holly died in his arms. The following day-Friday, Ray brought the usual cup of tea then slipped away into his trance state. Birds could be heard singing outside the bedroom as the teacher, Mentor, controlled Ray and gave me these words that I wrote down, and later gave to Holly's husband.

151

POEM FOR A FRIEND

A friend of yours you hold so dear,
Has now come to join us here.
Against pain and anguish she did truly fight,
To try to make her spirit bright.
On that sandy shore to greet,
Many friends her soul did meet.
She sends you greetings from above,
And gives you thanks for all your love.
Although you knew her for just a while,
You helped turn tears into a smile.
Now she knows what she saw was true,
The sand was shivering and the sky was blue.
Do not hold any grief in your heart,
For new life she now does start.
One day a message to you she will send,
Telling that life does never end.
To one that travelled with her on the way,
She would to him have me say,
The love that we shared nothing will sever
I will love you darling for ever and ever.

As Ray said in the preface, many people respond to the healing that is given, and make remarkable recoveries. Experiences like those of Charri and Holli give me the strength to continue even though some have reached the time to 'go home'. Since Franz, Phillipe and other invisible friends were doctors when they lived on earth, they very often help me in my healing work. They often suggest which type of healing is best for the patient and also suggest what natural remedies would be best. The more healing I do, the better I feel. I cannot claim to feel the pains of the patients -rather the opposite, for I am sure that I too benefit from those healing energies that are transmitted through me. Just as many of the family have benefited from Ray's hypno-therapy, they often come to me when they feel down in health. This seems to contradict the thought that familiarity breeds contempt.

In the preface, my husband told of the many 'coincidences that have happened in our lives together. Oliver tells me that he died on his wedding anniversary. My mother died on my father's birthday. A friend in Gibraltar told us how his mother sent for all the family, informing them that she would die at seven that same day. The mother was able to say good-bye to her family and did vacate her earthly body at exactly seven O clock. Other friends tell us of similar stories and I wonder whether readers have noticed that often their friends or relatives seem to have some control over the day or hour that they 'go home'?

Ray is now sixty six and I am sixty one. I pray that we both have the strength to continue to try to be of service. As the physical side of our relationship diminishes, a greater love seems to replace it. This is a love that I am sure we can take with us when it is time for us to 'go home'. If both our lives are similar in length to those in the group, we will be working for many more years yet. May I too thank those who have been willing to listen and hope that they have enjoyed reading this, the second book.

Before I bring this postscript to an end I feel that I must mention the fact that I always carry with me a photograph of Sai Baba. During one of the healing sessions, Holly claimed to have seen him. I feel that anyone who devotes their life to the welfare of others, deserves respect. If we ever did go to India to be in his presence, I'm sure he would say, "Why have you come here when you are needed in your own country". May you all in your work receive the same joy and comfort that I have been given. I would like to say a thank you to all those who helped us during our tours in England. I did remind Oliver Lodge that some people do want to listen. Maybe that is why he has chosen as the title of this book, "For those who are willing to listen-read on". Even though I may not meet you all in earthly life, I hope that I may meet you in one of those infinite levels of consciousness and if I had to choose a concluding song title it would be the same one that Oliver used——"We'll meet again-don't know where-don't know when, but I know we'll meet again some sunny day.

I will continue with my work and play.

God Bless You All.

June Smith.